A NEAR SYMPATHY

A Near Sympathy

The Timeless Quaker Wisdom of John Woolman

Michael L. Birkel

Friends United Press
Richmond, Indiana

Book design: Shari Pickett Veach

Cover art: Permission to use this illustration has been given by the Quaker Tapestry at Kendal. The Quaker Tapestry is a community textile of 77 embroidery panels made by 4,000 people from 15 countries. Further information can be obtained from: The Quaker Tapestry Exhibition & Tearooms, Friends Meeting House, Stramongate, Kendal, Cumbria, LA9 4BH England UK; Telephone and Fax: +44 (0) 1539 722975; http://www.quaker-tapestry.co.uk; Email info@quaker-tapestry.co.uk

Library of Congress Cataloging-in-Publication Data

Birkel, Michael Lawrence.
   A near sympathy : the timeless Quaker wisdom of John Woolman / Michael L. Birkel.
      p. cm.
   Includes bibliographical references.
   ISBN 0-944350-63-1 (alk. paper)
      1. Woolman, John, 1720-1772. 2. Society of Friends--Doctrines. I. Title.

BX7795.W7B57 2003
289.6'092--dc21
[B]
                                                    2002041673

For Gwen

Contents

Acknowledgments ix

Introduction xi

Chapter 1: Integrity and Love 1

Chapter 2: Worship 29

Chapter 3: Scripture 39

Chapter 4: Suffering and Redemption 57

Chapter 5: Nurturing Empathy 69

Chapter 6: Engaging the World 85

Closing Thoughts: To Take Heed to Our Own Spirits 113

Group Discussion Guide 117

.

Acknowledgments

I t takes a community to write a book, so my thanks are due to many. I first learned of John Woolman from vocal ministry in Campus Monthly Meeting in Wilmington, Ohio, where I initially encountered Friends. Later Hugh Barbour was my mentor in John Woolman, as he has been in so many aspects of Quaker history. I have taught John Woolman in classrooms, workshops, and retreats over the years, and I am grateful for all these opportunities. The writing of this book began during a sabbatical, for which I am thankful to Earlham College. My gratitude is deep to those who read and commented on various chapters. These include family members: my wife Gwen Halsted, our daughter Anna Margaret, and my father Francis Birkel. They also include colleagues past and present—Hugh Barbour, Mary Garman, Stephen Heiny, Paul Lacey—and my friends David Garman and Brad Stull. Thanks to all of you for your enduring support. Many thanks also to Barbara Mays, editor of Friends United Press, who patiently taught me how to write for a wider audience than the scholarly community to whom most of my previous writing had been directed.

Introduction

> I was led to meditate on the manifold difficulties of these Indians,…and a near sympathy with them was raised in me; and my heart being enlarged in the love of Christ, I thought that the affectionate care of a good man for his only brother in affliction does not exceed what I then felt for that people.
>
> —*Journal* of John Woolman

This moment in history feels chaotic to many people. One by one, illusions of security have slowly been whittled away. The financial market has become unstable. Many people fear they cannot count on their planned retirement income. Neither old nor young are secure: escalating violence in our schools means that many of our children are not safe. The terrorist attacks of September 11, 2001 are the epitome of our turmoil: if ever we were secure, we no longer are. Fear threatens to envelope us, but in this crisis lies an opportunity to be transformed. Sadly, the response of the United States for the most part to this chaos has been to grasp for ever-tighter security, to keep things as we prefer to believe they once were. In a crisis that invites us to deep change, our society is spending vast resources to try to stay the same. At such a moment, we need models of courageous people who took risks to move beyond fear in order to love others who were outside their immediate circle or culture. We need to listen intently to those voices of people, past and present, who can teach us about the inner work that liberates us from our fears and who can point us to a vision of a world transformed.

Although he lived in eighteenth-century New Jersey, in the little town of Mt. Holly, the colonial American Quaker John Woolman speaks eloquently to our moment. He ministers spiritually to our insecurity. His activism shows us we can change society. His life gives guidance for discovering the areas that are ours to work on, and he shows us ways to find hope and inward peace around issues that are not our particular responsibility. Although—and in fact, because—he lived fully present to the needs of his historical situation, his wisdom transcends that era and reaches out to ours.

This book is an invitation to a conversation with John Woolman on the inner life. The words of this abolitionist, mystic, and gentle, yet radical, social reformer strike a chord in the heart of readers, crossing the barriers of time, culture, and the changes in the English language that separate him from us. He lived his faith with an integrity that opens his readers to new possibilities for their own lives. His writings explain the courageous ethical stands he took, many of which jarred his contemporaries into realization of the injustices they were perpetrating—for example, when visiting a slavekeeper, he insisted on paying the slaves for their services. John Woolman tells of his outward activities and reflects on the way the world is and the way it could be. He models what he calls "a near sympathy," which is a way to engage in love those whom we would otherwise be tempted to regard as different and threatening. His *Journal* records his profound religious experiences. By example, his earnest self-examination gently invites readers into reflection on their own lives. By its gentle honesty, the *Journal* breathes a kind of hospitality for the reader. We feel beckoned to the spiritual life.

READING AS AN ACT OF FRIENDSHIP

Some of my most cherished friends are people who lived long ago. Since my training was in the history of ancient Christianity, some of my friendships cross boundaries not only of centuries but of millennia. I still turn to these people, including John Woolman, for guidance, and I feel cared for by them in a way that I call friendship.

It is one thing to admire a long-dead author, but by "friendship" I mean more than admiration. I am referring to an experience of feeling known by each other. A text can befriend us when we see it as psychologically and spiritually true to our own deepest personal experiences. John Woolman's teachings on simplicity have this ring of truth for me, and they have changed my life. His reflections on suffering have strengthened me to endure the death of loved ones, and they have enabled me to find meaning amid life's pain.

To call someone who died over two hundred years ago a friend is an act of imagination on our part, but the imagining makes something real happen. This act of imagining mediates yet is at the same time mediated by divine presence. Early Quaker George

Fox says we come to "know one another in that which is eternal."* To use an expression from John Woolman, we can say that his words "reach the pure witness" in us. They appeal to the Inward Light that verifies them. And what better thing can a friend do than bring us in touch with God?

Another great thing about having friends is that they introduce you to their friends, and the circles of friendship widen. Because John Woolman is my friend, and because he introduced me to his friend, the ancient prophet Jeremiah, I have come to know Jeremiah in a new way. When John Woolman read Jeremiah, he felt known by him in that same way I feel known by John Woolman when I read his words. Jeremiah described John Woolman's condition and spoke to it. His words mediated divine presence to John Woolman.

John Woolman is my friend, but I do not expect a friend to be in full agreement with me on every matter. Nor do I emulate John Woolman as some people do their heroes. But John Woolman has influenced my life dramatically. Because of my friendship with John Woolman, who spoke eloquently for moderate labor and for a simple life, I have chosen to work less than full time, to leave time to be with my family and to cultivate my spiritual life. His words on simplicity have led me to limit the

---

* George Fox, Letter 149, p. 114 in *The Power of the Lord is Over All: The Pastoral Letters of George Fox*, Introduced and edited by T. Canby Jones (Richmond, IN: Friends United Press, 1989.)

impact of the media in my house. His encouragement to live "in accordance with the design of creation" has inspired me to eat low on the food chain and to conserve the earth's resources. His words on worship have deepened my experience of Quaker worship in powerful ways. John Woolman has taught me to read scripture in a way that opens me to the presence of the Spirit who gave them forth. He has shown me the power of imagination as a spiritual discipline. John Woolman has opened to me new meanings of the cross, inviting me to participate in divine purpose. His integrated life challenges me to integrate the inward life of devotion and the outward life of the activist for justice and peace. My gratitude to my friend from Mt. Holly is profound.

Still, I neither try to copy him, nor do I go to him for approval in everything I do. I wear dyed clothing. I have used the English postal service. I also sing in a chorus, and I gained great spiritual benefit from singing the Brahms *Requiem* recently. Singing Brahms's gorgeous musical setting of biblical texts on death, the frailty of life, and divine comfort was nothing less than a transcendent experience. It brought me to grief and through grief to a sense of triumph over death through God's grace. Yet, for all his openness to other religious traditions, I suspect John Woolman was too much a product of his times to approve of a fellow Quaker like me singing in a symphony chorus. But this does not trouble me, nor does it endanger our friendship. We have come to know one another in that which is eternal. To use his expression, I feel "a near sympathy" with John Woolman.

THE SHAPE OF THIS BOOK

These essays explore different aspects of John Woolman's understanding of religious life, yet there is a larger pattern to them. The first chapter begins by looking at his central conviction that the inward life of love and devotion and the outward life of enacting justice are intricately united. John Woolman's life integrated the two in an exemplary way, for his day or any since. Love and justice are the impetus of the testimonies, the traditional Quaker ethical stands. Just as John Woolman integrated the inward and outward life, he also found that the testimonies were integrated. When he wrote that he was convinced true religion embraces both inward and outward aspects, he recounted that he was prepared for this insight by experiences of meeting for worship and by reading the Bible. So chapters two and three look at John Woolman's understanding of worship and his approach to reading the Bible, especially the prophets who were such an inspiration for him. Both chapters four and five examine complex passages from John Woolman's *Journal*. You may need to exercise some patience as I unravel these complicated texts, but it is worth the effort. Chapter four explores John Woolman's experience of bearing the cross. This chapter focuses on a vision he experienced toward the end of his life that revealed the depth of his union with the suffering oppressed. Chapter five focuses on a passage in which he describes the experience of spiritual transformation from a life focused on selfish gain to one of love of God and, as he put it, a "near sympathy" for others. The final chapter considers the legacy of John Woolman for contemporary readers. It looks at practical tools for engaging others in the quest for implementing justice, since John Woolman was not simply a theoretician of the just society but also modeled a way to interact with other people to change the wider world.

In these chapters, I seek to write primarily as a teacher for general readers rather than as a specialist for other specialists, so I have kept footnotes and other scholarly apparatus at a minimum. In order to let John Woolman speak for himself as much as possible, I have been generous with quotations from his writings.*

To simplify references, numbers in parentheses refer to the critical edition of John Woolman's *Journal* and longer essays:

Moulton, Phillips P., editor. *The Journal and Major Essays of John Woolman*. (New York: Oxford University Press, 1971; reprinted Richmond, IN: Friends United Press, 1989).

Numbers in italics in parentheses refer to an older edition, which also contained his shorter essays:

Gummere, Amelia Mott, editor. *The Journal and Essays of John Woolman*. (New York: Macmillan, 1922)

---

* No single work can do justice to the richness and complexity of John Woolman's religious genius. My hope is that these essays shed some light on John Woolman's understanding of the inward life. Other scholars have explored John Woolman and his era from a variety of angles. Jack Marietta has reshaped our understanding of John Woolman's context within a reformation in colonial Quakerism. J. William Frost has illuminated the Quaker family in that era. Michael Heller has explored John Woolman's rhetoric, which he has perceptively named "soft persuasion." Phillips Moulton has increased our appreciation of John Woolman's ethics. Sterling Olmsted has enlarged our understanding of John Woolman's views on economics. Henry Cadbury's painstaking account of John Woolman's final months in England is a model of perceptive history. This volume stands indebted to the insights of all these scholars.

Chapter 1

Integrity and Love

To act continually with integrity of heart above all narrow or selfish motives is a sure token of our being partakers of that salvation which God hath appointed for walls and bulwarks, and is, beyond all contradiction, a more happy situation than can ever be promised by the utmost reach of art and power united, not proceeding from heavenly wisdom. (204)

John Woolman is attractive to contemplatives and to activists, and rightly so, since he offers inspiration to both camps. "Camps" is unfortunately a good way to describe the two groups, since religious groups often split along this divide and do a kind of polite battle with one another. Each group claims its approach closer to Truth and wishes the other side would simply smarten up.

But John Woolman does not take sides on this issue. His life embraced the inward life of the contemplative and the outward life of the social reformer. He saw no separation between the two. His example calls both sides to a deeper commitment without asking them to abandon either path.

Traditional Quaker journals follow a typical pattern of organization: the journalist recounts intimations of closeness to God while a child, a period of youthful waywardness, a turning point or convincement, a call to ministry, and an account of his or her life in the ministry. John Woolman conforms to this pattern. In his *Journal* he writes of a significant turning point in his life. The first page of the *Journal* describes an experience of "the operations of divine love" that occurred before he reached the age of seven:

> as I went from school one Seventh Day, I remember, while my companions went to play by the way, I went forward out of sight; and sitting down, I read the twenty-second chapter of the Revelations: "He showed me a river of water, clear as crystal, proceeding out of the throne of God and the Lamb, etc." And in reading it my mind was drawn to seek after that pure habitation which I then believed God had prepared for his servants. The place where I sat and the sweetness that attended my mind remains fresh in my memory. (23)

The *Journal* then tells of a period of adolescent waywardness in which his "chief study" was "the art of foolish jesting." Frankly, his waywardness seems fairly tame by the standards of his day or ours*. He nonetheless found it a struggle to commit himself fully

---

*If lightheartedness is a serious sin, then I for one am in big trouble, but John Woolman did not leave behind all lightness of life when he committed himself to the spiritual life. The following story from the *Memorials of Rebecca Jones*, shows that some twenty years after he left his youthfull follies behind him, John Woolman still had a light side to him. It is delightful to imagine him walking into Rebecca Jones' house, smiling broadly and shaking the snow off his clothes, announcing that he felt he had earned his breakfast. William Allinson tells the story this way, offering us a lovely snapshot of John Woolman:

to a religious life. The following passage recounts his next stage, as his use of the word "convinced" suggests. The experience itself was clearly decisive for John Woolman. It is equally important to note the content of this convincement, because this passage describes what he understood to be the central truths of the religious life:

> I kept steady to meetings, spent First Days after noon chiefly in reading the Scriptures and other good books, and was early convinced in my mind that true religion consisted in an inward life, wherein the heart doth love and reverence God the Creator and learn to exercise true justice and goodness, not only toward all men but also toward the brute creatures; that as the mind was moved on an inward principle to love God as an invisible, incomprehensible being, on the same principle it was moved to love him in all his manifestations in the visible world; that as by his breath the flame of life was kindled in all animal and sensitive creatures, to say we love God as unseen and at the same time exercise cruelty toward the least creature moving by his life, or by life derived from him, was a contradiction in itself. (28)

On the night succeeding the Second Quarterly Meeting-day, in the Second month, probably about the year 1762, a great fall of snow occurred, which was the next morning piled up by an eddy half way up the door and window of our friends in Drinker's alley, who were apprehensive that they might not be able to make their way through the snow drifts to Quarterly Meeting. R. Jones opened the door to sweep the snow from the step, and found to her surprise, the pavement cleared, and a path made down the alley to Front street. Whilst she was preparing the morning repast, John Woolman entered, saying that he thought he had earned his breakfast. Having spent the previous night at Reuben Haines', in High Street near Fourth, he arose early, and remembering the lone sisters in their need, and every ready for an appropriate labor of love, however humble, he took with him from his lodgings, a snow shovel, proceeded (wading through the deep snow from Second street downwards,) and cleared a path from R. Jones' house to the Bank Meeting near Mulberry street. After breakfast he made a passage to Second street for the benefit of the scholars. (*Memorials of Rebecca Jones*, compiled by William J. Allinson. Second edition. Philadelphia: Henry Longstreth, 1849, p. 36.)

True religion is both inward and outward. The same principle moves the human spirit in both directions. The most repeated word in this passage is "love"—love for God, love for neighbor, love for all God's creation. All these types of love come from the same source and are intimately interwoven: where we find one, we find the others—at least when religion is most true to itself. John Woolman may have meant for the attentive reader to hear an echo from the First Epistle of John (4:20), where it says that those who do not love a brother or sister they have not seen cannot love God who is unseen. John Woolman equates love for others with justice and goodness, a clue as to what love looks like in the visible world. John Woolman identifies the practices that led to this insight: the experience of communal worship and the reading of spiritual books, especially the Bible.

LOVE AT THE CENTER

As John Woolman reflected on the effects of his experience of convincement, love continued as the center. Love was the natural result of spiritual growth.

> As I lived under the cross and simply followed the openings of Truth, my mind from day to day was more enlightened. ...While I silently ponder on that change wrought in me, I find no language equal to it nor any means to convey to another a clear idea of it. I looked upon the works of God in this visible creation and an awfulness covered me; my heart was tender and often contrite, and a universal love to my fellow creatures increased in me. This will be understood by such who have trodden in the same path.

The effects of this love were evident, at least to those who followed the same spiritual path, which is what his reference to the white stone and new name of Revelation 2:17 suggests.

> Some glances of real beauty may be seen in their faces who dwell in true meekness. There is a harmony in the sound of that voice to which divine love gives utterance, and some appearance of right order in their temper and conduct whose passions are fully regulated. Yet all these do not fully show forth that inward life to such who have not felt it, but this white stone and new name is known rightly to such only who have it. (29)

I have seen this meekness in the face of an old monk who was too humble to want his name recorded here. We met years ago when I was a visiting his monastery to pray with his community and to use their wonderful library of monastic writings on the spiritual life. Simply to be in his presence was a gift; it radiated a quiet joy. He dwelt in meekness and harmony. The memory of meeting him is an enduring blessing, and I can turn to that memory and feel that blessing renewed.

People whose lives have been transformed by love recognize the signs of this transformation in others. They do not form a secret club, which would exclude others, because the love that flows from God is inclusive. John Woolman spoke of this love in terms echoing the creation story in Genesis, which speaks of human beings as created in the image and likeness of God. John Woolman suggested that love constitutes this likeness. What makes us like God is our capacity to love. Since this love is like

God's love, it has no boundaries. Our experience of God's love moves us to love others.

> For as God's love is universal, so where the mind is sufficiently influenced by it, it begets a likeness of itself and the heart is enlarged towards all. (202)

For John Woolman, this love that God begets in the heart is none other than the love of Christ, which produces a willingness to suffer redemptively for the sake of others.

> It is with Reverence that I acknowledge the Mercies of our Heavenly Father, who, in Infinite Love, did visit me in my Youth, and wrought a Belief in me, that through true Obedience a State of inward Purity may be known in this Life; in which we may love Mankind in the same Love with which our Redeemer loveth us, and therein learn Resignation to endure Hardships, for the real Good of others. (*384*)

Although this love is a divine gift, it requires maintenance. The upkeep of love includes interior watchfulness, so that we are aware of any temptation to allow a selfish orientation to return to power in our lives.

> When we love the Lord with all our Hearts, and his Creatures in his Love, we are then preserved in Tenderness both toward Mankind and the Animal Creation; but if another Spirit gets Room in our Minds, and we follow it in our Proceedings, we are then in the Way of disordering the Affairs of Society. (*489*)

Spiritual vigilance, watching over our thoughts and motivations, can preserve us in divine love. Otherwise, lesser forms of love can deceive us. Of these, John Woolman mentioned two especially. One is the love of this world, or, echoing the Epistle of James (4:4), the friendship of this world. This is opposed to the friendship of God, which is characterized thus: "the wisdom that is from above is first pure, then peaceable, gentle, and easy to be entreated, full of mercy and good fruits, without partiality, and without hypocrisy (James 3:17)." The friendship of this world, as understood by John Woolman's reading of James, is motivated by narrow self-interest and by concern for reputation with the wealthy and powerful:

> acting contrary to present outward interest from a motive of divine love and in regard to truth and righteousness, and thereby incurring the resentments of people, opens the way to a treasure better than silver and to a friendship exceeding the friendship of men. (46)

Another, lesser species of love is what John Woolman calls "natural affection." It is instinctive and ultimately a kind of self-preservation. Like the friendship of this world, it is not self-giving. Unlike Christ's love, it is not willing to suffer to redeem.

> Natural affection needs a careful examination. Operating upon us in a soft manner, it kindles desires of love and tenderness, and there is danger of taking it for something higher. To me it appears an instinct like that which inferior creatures have; each of them, we see, by the ties of nature love self best. That which is a part of

self they love by the same tie or instinct. In them it in some measure does the offices of reason, by which among other things, they
watchfully keep and orderly feed their helpless offspring. Thus
natural affection appears to be a branch of self-love, good in the
animal race, in us likewise with proper limitations, but otherwise is
productive of evil by exciting desires to promote some by means
prejudicial to others. (198)

This can seem like a hard lesson. As a parent, how con I
possibly love anyone else the way that I love my children? My
love for them, however, should not tempt me to perpetrate injustice to others so that my children can have "a better life." The
love God gives to those who are open to it is universal in its
scope. It embraces the unloved who are pushed to the margins of
society and is zealous for justice for all God's creation. God's love
is for all, but at the same time God's love is for justice for all. The
claims of God on the faithful to behave in accordance with justice may appear to go against the grain, or even violate good
manners, in human communities that have injustice embedded
in their very structures. John Woolman successfully managed to
advocate such justice without succumbing to the pitfall of self-
righteousness because he kept his focus on God's love as the center of his encounter with others.

Shortly after the tragic events of September 11, 2001, I had
a conversation with a friend whose comments showed just this
distinction between a narrow and a universal love. We were reflecting on the varied responses to the tragedy. Pacifists were more
convinced than ever of the futility of violence, yet most of our
co-citizens were eager for revenge. She suggested that these op-

posite reactions "depended on where you think you live. If, fundamentally, you think you live in the United States of America and just happen to have to share the planet with others, then you will have one response. You want to protect your country and to eliminate its enemies. But if you think you live in the world, and the United States is the piece of that world where you happen to live, then your response will be one of care for all of God's children. You are deeply saddened by these tragedies and you want to prevent additional violence throughout the whole world. You want to protect all people." My friend was not limited by the "natural affection" to which patriotism tempts us. Her love was wide enough to include all who are created in God's image.

Love Enacted: 'Exercising True Justice and Goodness'

To John Woolman, the Quaker testimonies were the outgrowth of the transformed life. A life centered in love would be drawn, as a matter of course, to a life of honesty and integrity, of peace, of simplicity, and of commitment to human equality. As John Woolman integrated the inward and outward qualities of the religious life, he experienced the interwoven nature of the testimonies. Flowing from the same divine principle, they were deeply united. True simplicity led to peace. The pursuit of wealth and luxury, he believed, inevitably led to involvement in oppression, which violated the testimony of equality and bred conditions for war. Since human greed, as he saw it, was the root of injustice and violence, the call to lead a simple life lay at the root of his understanding of exercising true justice and goodness.

PROVIDENCE—CONFIDENCE IN DIVINE CARE

A life of simplicity grew from a trust that God would provide. It was John Woolman's firm belief that God rewards those who take the risk of trusting in divine Providence:

> as people attend to his heavenly instruction and put their trust in him, he provides for them in all parts where he gives them a being. (114)

He found precedent for this in the lives of biblical figures, who "afforded instruction" for those in later ages:

> Abraham was called of God to leave his country and kindred, to sojourn amongst strangers. Through famine and danger of death he was forced to flee from one kingdom to another. He at length not only had assurance of being the father of many nations, but became a mighty prince. Gen. 23:6. (206)

Likewise, he noted, Jacob, Joseph, David, and others serve as further examples. Although they all faced afflictions and endured "grievous sufferings," God preserved their lives. The adversities that they survived were themselves by providential design, so that they might learn compassion for others in similar straits.

> The Most High acquaints them that his love is not confined, but extends to the stranger, and to excite their compassion, reminds them of times past: "Ye were strangers in the land of Egypt." Deut. 10:19. Again, "Thou shalt not oppress a stranger, for ye know the heart of a stranger, seeing ye were strangers in the land of Egypt." Ex. 23:9. (207)

God's providence, John Woolman insisted, was not confined to the distant past:

> He who sent ravens to feed Elijah in the wilderness, and increased the poor widow's small remains of meal and oil, is now as attentive to the necessities of his people as ever, that when he numbers us with his people and saith, "Ye are my sons and daughters" [2 Cor. 6:18] — no greater happiness can be desired by them who know how gracious a Father he is. (250)

Simplicity was not a hazardous undertaking. God responded to human trust with care. There have been people throughout history who have been called to a life a radical simplicity, the desert mothers and fathers of the early monastic movement, Francis of Assisi, Dorothy Day, Mother Teresa, and many others. Most of us are not given this special calling. Still, we are challenged to trust God's assurances to provide for us. What might that trust look like for us?

LIVING IN ACCORDANCE WITH THE DESIGN OF CREATION

The core of John Woolman's understanding of simplicity and justice is this: the world belongs to the One who made it; since it was made with a particular purpose in mind, human beings find their own fulfillment when they live in accordance with that purpose.

Pure wisdom was one of John Woolman's favorite expressions to refer to God's nature. The world, according to the book of Proverbs, was created in wisdom, who was God's partner in creation when the boundaries of sea and land and of day and night were established. For John Woolman, pure wisdom fixed the boundaries of labor, so that people did not work too much or make others work too much on their behalf. In his *Journal* he described the experience of setting aside our selfish desires and discovering that wisdom sets boundaries to all our wants. Unbounded desires engender greed that leads to oppression. But the experience of bounded desires is not one of prohibition or restriction: once people have the experience of their soul's true desire, other things simply are not as interesting anymore. Maybe it is like being a compulsive collector of third-rate paintings and then discovering the works of a real genius. What was once a passion is no longer appealing. Pure wisdom sets boundaries to otherwise disordered desires.

This process of reorienting desires enables people to see God's nature as love, and it brings them to love others, particularly those whom they had been dehumanizing through oppression. In turn, this experience of love brings them to commit themselves to make society just and righteous. This process is for John Woolman the fundamental spiritual transformation.

This experience was so central to his understanding of the religious life that he did not hesitate to call it redemptive. He spoke, for example, of those "who are so redeemed from the love of the world as to possess nothing in a selfish spirit," (250) and said elsewhere that "to be redeemed from all the remains of selfishness" was "to have a universal regard to our fellow creatures, and love them as [God] loves them." (248) God as pure wisdom invited people into this redemptive love.

John Woolman wrote, "The Creator of the earth is the owner of it." This Creator "gave us being thereon, and our nature requires nourishment which is the produce of it." Because God "is kind and merciful, we as [God's] creatures, while we live answerable to the design of our creation, are so far entitled to a convenient subsistence that no [one] may justly deprive us of it." (239) God's kindness and mercy imply that the design of our creation has mercy and kindness woven into its fabric. The universe is designed benevolently and justly, with the intention that life flourish.

One name John Woolman gave to this design is "harmony." In music harmony derives from right proportions and is an expression of beauty; for John Woolman harmony is found in right relationships and is beautiful. The human body finds harmony in the right proportion of labor and rest. Overwork results in bodily discord, which must be resolved before real rest can occur.

> I have observed that too much Labour not only makes the Understanding dull, but so intrudes upon the Harmony of the Body, that after ceasing from our Toil, we have another to pass through, before we can be so composed as to enjoy the Sweetness of Rest. (388)

This harmonious design for the human body is paralleled in the Creator's design for social harmony.

> How agreeable to the true harmony of Society, is that exhortation of the Apostle "Look not every man on his own things, but every man also on the things of others. Let this mind be in you which was also in Christ Jesus." (447)

Greed disrupts this harmony, giving rise to envy and ill feeling and opening the way to the oppression of slavery. The results are the raw materials for war.

> In true gospel simplicity free from all wrong use of things, a spirit which breathes peace and good will is cherished... A covetous mind which seeks opportunity to exalt itself is a great enemy to true harmony in a country. Envy and grudging usually accompany this disposition, and it tends to stir up its likeness in others. And where this disposition ariseth so high as to embolden us to look upon honest, industrious men as our own property during life, and to keep them to hard labour to support us in those customs which have not their foundation in right reason, or to use any means of oppression, a haughty spirit is cherished on one side and the desire of revenge frequently on the other, till the inhabitants of the land are ripe for great commotion and trouble; and thus luxury and oppression have the seeds of war and desolation in them. (227-228)

Just as there is a disharmonious "wrong use of things" that leads to destruction, so also there is a "right use of things" that is in harmony with the benevolent design of creation. There is a kind of divine ecology at work. Creation is designed for particular purposes. If unnecessary luxuries and what Woolman called "the desire of outward greatness" (wealth, power, prestige) were laid aside, and if people attended to the right use of things, there would be employment for everyone, and only moderate labor would be required. This is "that use of things prescribed by our Redeemer, and confirmed by his example" (240). He wrote of "the necessity of attending singly to divine wisdom ... thereby to be directed in the right use of things, in opposition to the customs of the times" (247).

One feature of the right use of things is moderate labor. John Woolman's notion of moderate labor was unusual for his day, or ours. He did not conform to what is called the Protestant work ethic. Labor is healthful and contributes to our well-being. His era was agricultural and pre-industrial, and so most labor was physical. For him, labor was not an evil; he did not speak of work as the unfortunate result of original sin. It was part of the design of the creation. It is too much labor that is the problem. When desires are out of hand, people want too many things. To get these things, they either have to overwork themselves, which does not leave them the energy or the frame of mind to cultivate a spiritual life, or they make others overwork on their behalf. This leads to oppression, injustice, and slavery.

He wrote approvingly of those among the wealthy landowners who "live in the spirit of charity" and inform themselves about the living conditions of their tenants. As a result, these particular wealthy people "regulate their demands" in a way "agreeable to universal love," despite social pressures and permissions to do otherwise. For example, they charge less than what the market would allow for rents or interest on loans, and they pay better wages to their employees. Such persons, said John Woolman, do the right thing as a matter of principle, and so "do good to the poor without placing it as an act of bounty." They do the right thing because justice requires it, not because they want to be recognized and publicly thanked for it. This in turn "tends to open the channel to moderate labor in useful affairs," in accordance with pure wisdom (239).

John Woolman said that when we demand too much labor of others in order to serve our own selfish desires for luxury, "we invade their rights as inhabitants of that world of which a good and gracious God is proprietor, under whom we are tenants" (240). Wealthy landowners can be tempted to think of themselves as above their tenants, yet here John Woolman reminds us that all of us are equally tenants under God.

With vivid imagery he described the risks of immoderate labor:

> To labor too hard or cause others to do so, that we may live conformable to customs which Christ our Redeemer contradicted by his example in the days of his flesh [that is, Jesus lived a simple life], and which are contrary to divine order, is to manure a soil for propagating an evil seed in the earth. (247)

The danger of wealth is that it brings power, which can be misused. John Woolman described oppression as the "weight of misapplied power" (243) and identified it as the evil seed just mentioned.

> and here oppression, carried on with worldly policy and order, clothes itself with the name of justice and becomes like a seed of discord in the soil; and ... so the seeds of war swell and sprout and grow and become strong, till much fruits are ripened. (255)

Here we might hear an echo of the Epistle of James in the New Testament. Wars come from unbridled desires.

WOOLMAN'S DECISION NOT TO PURSUE WEALTH

John Woolman practiced what he preached. When he was in his early twenties, others perceived he was talented for a career in business, but he chose instead the humbler lot of a tailor. He had apprenticed himself to a shopkeeper to learn business, but then felt led in another direction. He wrote that his mind "through the power of Truth was in a good degree weaned from the desire of outward greatness," and that "a humble person with divine blessing might live on a little," and that

> where the heart was set on greatness, success in business did not satisfy the craving, but that in common with an increase of wealth the desire of wealth increased. (35)

Why does success in business fail to satisfy the craving? John Woolman would say the craving is ultimately misdirected. Human beings have an inherent thirst for the presence of God. Trusting something so intangible is frightening, so we try to substitute something else to quench that thirst. We cannot satisfy a thirst for the infinite with something finite. So we end up wanting more money and more success. No amount is ever enough. Having begun to understand this, John Woolman took up the life of a tailor, a manageable kind of work. This work freed him to devote more time to the inward life and travel under religious concerns, especially on behalf of the oppressed in his day.

Greed is alive and well in our society, but I suspect most people who will read John Woolman or this book about him do not have an uncontrolled lust for riches at the center of their lives. Yet we lead very busy lives. Our "desire for outward great-ness" is not a drive for wealth but a concern for what John Woolman called "reputation." We are so busy because we yearn for a certain status that comes from busy-ness itself as well as from the particular tasks that keep us busy.

In some ways our era has reversed a millennia-old trend. In the ancient world, one's status was measured by how much lei-sure one had. Lavish banquets and luxurious hunting trips, for example, were a sign of high social standing. Our era has its ex-travagant vacations and conspicuous consumption, but for many of us it is our busy-ness that affords us standing among our peers. We fill up our lives with activities and committees that commu-nicate our self-importance. The causes themselves—such as so-cial justice, peacemaking, and care of the environment—are wor-thy, but the net sum of them weighs many of us down.

My work is in education. Schools thrive on altruism and of-ten reward it with a kind of prestige. Altruism is good, but not when we make it a competitive sport or invest too much of our sense of worth in the prestige such busy-ness promises. A col-league of mine tells a story of two new teachers at our college. One was about to leave at the end of a long day but then noticed the other's office light was still on. Feeling he must not have worked hard enough, he returned to his office to do more. Mean-while the other person prepared to leave but noticed the first person still had his light on. So the second person went back to his office to do more work. On it went—a fitting parable for a culture of overwork.

By my own choice, I work less than full time at my school, but I care deeply about its mission. It is too easy for me to say "yes" to serve on an important committee or to overcommit myself to a project that is dear to my heart. As a result, I can find myself with less time to give to those parts of my life for which I decided to work less than full time, such as my family and my spiritual life. When, instead, I bear in mind the wisdom that John Woolman offers and resist the urge to take on more busyness, I experience the benefits of a more centered life. My interior well does not run dry but is replenished by more time for prayer and meditation. I am more fully present to my loved ones and to all my community.

In my own experience, the quest for a reputation as a good worker or valued colleague has the same root as greed. Both stem from an insufficient trust in God. The greedy person does not deeply trust God to provide for him or her and, therefore, gathers as many material possessions as possible. In a similar way, when I fail to trust God's acceptance of me as I am, I try to substitute the acceptance of others, and I overwork to achieve that acceptance. People, however, can never supply what only God can give, so the quest for a reputation or for status is and endless pursuit. No amount is ever enough; a temporal scratch cannot satisfy a divine itch. John Woolman's example is a gentle, persistent reminder that God will provide the acceptance I need. I do not have to look for it in serving on prestigious but demanding committees, or in my reputation among scholars of religion. To expect them to satisfy a need only God can meet is, in the long run, only an exercise in frustration.

An Exercise of Imagination

John Woolman hoped to persuade readers that his ideas on economic justice and simplicity are reasonable and true, but his writings are more than an appeal to reason alone. They are also an invitation to spiritual growth, to a change of heart. John Woolman invited readers to use not only their capacity to reason but also their ability to imagine. The imagination can be a spiritual practice that opens the way to an inward transformation that redeems us from the selfish spirit. John Woolman describes a scene and asks his readers to picture themselves there. More than mere visualization, it also is a matter of opening themselves up to the inward responses that are evoked by the scene they are picturing in their minds. Those inward responses may open the way to a perception of truth readers had not realized before, and that realization of truth may inspire a commitment to action.

Imagination opens the way to perceiving how those who bear the burden of injustice feel. It is an invitation to identify with them and to be in solidarity with them. This practice of imagination reaches what John Woolman calls the "pure witness" within people. This interior witness is of divine origin. It verifies the truth of those feelings and perceptions. It says, "Yes, this is true." As a result people are moved to love those whom their wider culture prefers to regard as unlovable. It convinces people of the need for justice.

The imaginative skills John Woolman advocates require us to sit attentively with the other reality we are trying to embrace with compassion through our imagination. This process takes time and practice. We might contrast this with media advertisements in our day. While they may look imaginative at one level, they do not invite us to exercise sustained attention. The average image in a television commercial lasts less than a second. Some suggest this experience creates a desire for incessant stimulation. It certainly does not promote the discipline of attention essential to the kind of imagination John Woolman is interested in. Such attentiveness is needed to imagine a situation in which injustice parades as justice, when oppression is acceptable, proper, and civil—when it is considered bad manners to think or act otherwise. Like the biblical prophets in whose footsteps he followed, John Woolman is more interested in morals than in manners.

Take a few moments now to exercise your imagination in this way. This is a scene common to newcomers to my little city in Indiana. These recent arrivals are indigenous people from the state of Oaxaca, Mexico. Spanish is the second language; Mixteca is their mother tongue. In their own country they are often scorned as *indios* and regarded as second-class citizens. Imagine, for a moment, their life:

You are cold. You live in a run-down mobile home, with no insulation against the winter cold that is so new to you. The only source of heat is a little kerosene stove. You live with nine other people in a space that four middle-class, United States citizens would consider crowded conditions. Unemployment and poverty back home have driven you to seek other possibilities, so you crossed the border into the United States. As an undocumented immigrant, you feel no protection of the law. This makes you easy prey for fraud from unscrupulous landlords, employers, and moneylenders. You are frightened. You are hungry. There is not enough food, so what there is you have given to your children. You discover that you are pregnant and wonder how you can provide for a growing family. You go to temporary agencies to find work. Some weeks there is work; other weeks there is none. You have learned that your mother, who lives back home in your village in Oaxaca and to whom you send money each payday, is sick. You are worried about her. You wish you could be there. If you were to visit her, though, it would be even harder to cross back into the United States. Since September 11, 2001, the border is increasingly militarized. You get a temporary job at minimum wage standing on your feet for twelve-hour shifts cutting vegetables in a refrigerated space for fast-food restaurants. Working in a large refrigerator is hard on you because you come from a tropical climate. Still, it is better than the past two weeks of no work at all. It is better than the battery factory and the burns you got from the chemicals when you worked there. People look at you with suspicion when you go shopping for groceries. Last month the Immigration and Naturalization Service raided a factory and deported fifty people, including your cousin and your brother-in-law. They had been in the United States longer than you and had been valuable guides on how to adjust to life in this foreign culture. You miss them and do not feel safe.

If you have chosen to receive this invitation to imagine, what feelings are you experiencing now? Does you heart connect with the life of this impoverished immigrant? Lawmakers and law enforcers often refer to such people as "illegal aliens." How does that term feel to you? Currently the United States is experiencing a revival of xenophobia, the fear of strangers. The Greek word in the New Testament for hospitality is *philoxenia*, which means "love of strangers." In the original Greek of the New Testament, the word for "stranger" also means "guest." As Christians, how do we exercise the hospitality the Bible asks of us?

Here are some of the things that John Woolman asks readers to imagine in his essay "A Plea for the Poor":

Imagine being in the situation of the poor laborers, people who are forced by circumstances to do the work of two or three people. Who, John Woolman asked, would not simplify their lives so as to make fewer demands, once they truly understood the reality of the poor?

Our blessed Redeemer, in directing us how to conduct one toward another, appeals to our own feeling: "Whatsoever ye would that other men should do to you, do ye even so to them." Now where such live in fullness on the labour of others, who have never had experience of hard labour themselves, there is often a danger of their not having a right feeling of the labourer's condition, and therefore of being disqualified to judge candidly in their case, as not knowing what they themselves would desire were they to labour hard from one year to another to raise the necessaries of life and pay large rents beside—that it's good for those who live in fullness to labour for tenderness of heart, and improve every opportunity of being acquainted with the hardships and fatigues of those who labour for their living, and [to] think seriously with themselves: Am I influenced with true charity in fixing all my demands? Have I no desire to support myself in expensive customs because my acquaintances live in those customs? Were I to labour as they do toward supporting them and their children in a station like mine, in such sort as they and their children labour for us, could I not on such a change, before I entered into agreements of rent or interest, name some costly articles now used by me or in my family which have no real use in them, the expense whereof might be lessened? And should I not in such case strongly desire the disuse of those needless expenses, that less answering their way of life the terms might be the easier to me? (241-42)

Over two centuries later, John Woolman's queries are still worthy of our attention. As we imagine ourselves in the situation of the poor, how does our standard of living look? What can we change about our patterns of consumption?

Imagine the thinking of the oppressed poor. When the poor laborer considers that the oppressive actions of the wealthy are socially acceptable, and "sees no means of redress in this world,"

how would the inward sighing of an innocent person ascend to the throne of that great, good Being, who created us all and hath a constant care over his creatures. ... By candidly considering these things, we may have some sense of the condition of innocent people overloaded by the wealthy. But he who toils one year after another to furnish others with wealth and superfluities, who labours and thinks, and thinks and labours, till by overmuch labor he is wearied and oppressed, such an one understands the meaning of that language: "Ye know the heart of a stranger, seeing ye were strangers in the land of Egypt [Exod. 23:9]." (243)

Notice what is happening with the biblical passage here. John Woolman is identifying the poor of his day with the ancient Hebrews toiling as slaves under their Egyptian overlords. What does this imply about the rich of John Woolman's day? They are identified with the oppressive slavekeepers of ancient Egypt—the villains. Usually when religious people read the scriptures, they like to identify themselves with the chosen people. Here John Woolman is inviting the wealthy to see themselves as the other side. This "angle" takes imagination because it is not the standard way of seeing yourself if you are privileged. The temptation is to think, "I am doing well in life, so God obviously likes me better." Sometimes we need to use our imagination to see the truth.

Imagine yourself in heaven. He challenges the excuse, "I am only making so much money so that I can give it to my children," noting that to give our children great wealth is to put them in the position to oppress others, which is dangerous for their own well being. If the wealthy think it will make them happy to leave their children in such danger, let them consider how they will feel after death. If they are in heaven, only goodness will make them happy, and so fostering conditions for injustice will not add to their celestial bliss. In "that state of being, ... there is no possibility of our taking delight in any thing contrary to the pure principle of universal love" (249).

Imagine an island. Suppose twenty families discover an uninhabited island and divide it equitably. Suppose nineteen of these first possessors provide for the future equitable distribution of their property "as best suited the convenience of the whole and tend[ing] to preserve love and harmony," and their descendants do likewise. Suppose also that the twentieth of these first settlers gives most of his lands to his favorite son making all the other sons his tenants and dependents, and that this favored son's heirs do the same. Other family members are reduced to tenants. Eventually there will be one great landlord over a twentieth of this island and the rest poor, oppressed people. John Woolman invited his readers to imagine this family-in-ruins to persuade them of this conclusion: if we were to trace the claim of the tenth of these great landlords down to the first and find the claim supported through these ten generations by legal documents, still "we could not admit a belief into our hearts that he had a right to so great a portion of land." When God gave life to these other people, now reduced to poverty, God gave them a right to the fruits of the earth, which cannot be denied or overridden by the legal claims of their landlord. They, "as creatures of the Most High God, possessor of heaven and earth, had a right to part of what this great claimer held, though they had no instruments [that is, legal documentation] to confirm their right" (262).

It does not require a lot of imagination on our part to see the implications of this scenario for people today living in a society that consumes so much of the world's resources.

Imagine a war. (Here I paraphrase so that we do not get tangled in his colonial syntax and miss the power of his words.)

Consider the great oppressions and tragedies brought on by nation making war on nation throughout history.

Consider the chaos in our own time brought on by the tremendous rush of so many people to become rich.

Consider how they pervert the true use of things, how they violate the purpose of creation, making war and shedding blood.

Consider how many people are employed in work to prepare for war, to support war.

Consider the great expense and effort required for maintaining armies.

Consider the miseries brought on by war, by combat.

Consider how much other people engaged in useful work have to overwork, to support not only themselves but also those in the armies and the demands of the consumptive lifestyle of their landlords.

Consider the hardships brought on by their having to work too hard, to support these others who are not productively engaged— while in the meantime others are making lifelong prisoners of people from distant lands, to force them to spend the rest of their lives in the terrible condition of slaves. (253)

Here again we see John Woolman as heir to the Letter of James: where do wars come from?

If we accept his invitation to imagine, John Woolman's words cry out for connection to today's situation. As I write, there is war or nearly war in Guatemala, Nigeria, Afghanistan, Colombia, and along the border between Pakistan and India. A voice cries out in Ramallah: Rachel and Hagar are weeping for their children. As I write, the United States government is trying to negotiate a ceasefire between Palestine and Israel but at the same time trying to stir up war fever against Iraq. As John Woolman noted, war making is intimately tied to moneymaking. War is so widespread in part because some hope to profit from it. In light of this he wrote the following, contrasting "business" as profit making with the business of being Christian:

> Thus oppression in the extreme appears terrible, but oppression in more refined appearances remains to be oppression, and where the smallest degree of it is cherished it grows stronger and more extensive: that to labor for a perfect redemption from this spirit of oppression is the great business of the whole family of Christ Jesus in this world. (262)

Chapter 2

Worship

From an inward purifying, and steadfast abiding under it, springs a
lively operative desire for the good of others. All faithful people
are not called the to the public ministry, but whoever are, are called
to minister to that which they have tasted and handled spiritually.
The outward modes of worship are various, but wherever men are
true ministers of Jesus Christ it is from the operation of his spirit
upon their hearts, first purifying them and thus giving them a feeling sense of the condition of others. (31)

John Woolman mentioned meeting for worship as the first
source of his convincement. Worship lay at the center of
John Woolman's life. As for Friends throughout history, for
John Woolman the experience of meeting for worship was manifold. Meeting for worship could be joyful, consoling, disturbing,
and revealing. Here Friends encountered their truest selves as
limitlessly loved by God. To come to that encounter they often
first had to come face to face with any illusions they might have
about themselves. These misperceptions could be many things,
but often they were centered in their understanding of their relationship to God.

SACRAMENTAL LANGUAGE

Communion. Like his Quaker contemporaries, John Woolman spoke of worship in sacramental terms. Other Christian bodies in colonial America observed the outward rituals of baptism with water and of communion with bread and cup. Quakers did not make use of such rituals, believing that worship in silence achieved the same goals toward which these rituals aspired. Silent worship was, they said, the worship about which Jesus spoke in the Gospel of John (4:24) when he said that God is a Spirit, and those who worship God must worship in spirit and in truth.

Christians who practiced the outward ritual of communion described their experience in several ways. For some it was the real presence of Christ. Some explained communion as a foretaste of the heavenly, messianic banquet. Communion strengthened the community as the body of Christ. Quakers experienced their unique form of worship, in which the community gathered and waited upon God in silence until words were given to share with the others, to be all these things as well. The living Christ was present, the faithful fed on this presence, and the bonds of the worshipping community were fortified.

In his essay "On Silent Worship," John Woolman wrote, "In real silent worship the soul feeds on that which is Divine." To worship in this way is to "partake of the table of the Lord," to experience the real presence of Christ, the living bread, which nourished the soul (*510*).

John Calvin and his theological heirs, unlike Catholics and Lutherans, refrained from the language of a physical presence of Christ in the bread. The body of Christ, said Calvin, ascended to heaven and was still there. Communion does not so much bring the physical body of Christ down to earth as it raises the believers to heaven where they could enjoy the presence of Christ. John Woolman agreed with Calvin that worship could lift the worshipers heavenward, though he did not use the language of sacramental communion to describe this experience. Instead, he alluded to the book of Revelation. The eighth chapter of that text begins:

> And when the Lamb had opened the seventh seal, there was silence in heaven about the space of half an hour. And I saw the seven angels who stood before God, seven trumpets were given to them. Another angel with a golden censer came and stood at the altar, to whom was a great quantity of incense to offer with the prayers of all saints on the golden altar that was before the throne. And the smoke of the incense, with the prayers of the saints, arose before God from the angel's hand. (Rev. 8:1-4)

John Woolman spoke of "pure inward prayer" as "the prayer of the saints" that "ariseth up and before the throne of God and the Lamb." (160) English Friend Elihu Robinson heard John Woolman speak in meeting for worship. In his unpublished diary he noted: "Our Friend John Woolman from Jersey . . . made several beautiful remarks in this meeting ... with respect to the benefit of true silence, and how incense ascended on the opening of the seventh seal, and there was silence in heaven for the space of half an hour" (*129*). The inward communion experienced in genuine worship in true silence carries worshipers to the heavenly throne.

In my own Quaker meeting a member described his communion experiences in worship as an inward priesthood. In the silence he would come to feel a sense of connection with other worshippers. He might feel led to go, in his heart while his body was still seated, from member to member of the worshipping community, offering communion. The elements of communion were not the usual bread and cup used in other churches. To one he might offer a flower, to another a candle, to another a bowl of fruit, as he felt led by the Holy Spirit. It felt, he said, like a walking prayer and a communion with the other worshippers and with God. This was his silent ministry to the gathered meeting.

Baptism. Among other Christian groups, water baptism was initiation into the church. Baptism was the entry into the body of Christ and opened the door to redemption. Friends in John Woolman's day at times spoke of worship as a baptizing experience. Just as other Christians regarded water baptism as an initiation into the community of the church, in meeting for worship Quakers experienced the possibility to enter inwardly into the life of the gathered community of worshippers. Such an experience was often difficult, even purgative, as Jesus himself suggested when he used baptismal language to describe the sufferings and death he would face:

> But Jesus said to them, "You do not know what you are asking. Are you able to drink the cup that I drink, or be baptized with the baptism that I am baptized with?" (Mark 10:38)

The apostle Paul similarly describes baptism as dying—and rising—with Christ (Romans 6:3): "Do you not know that all of us who have been baptized into Christ Jesus were baptized into his death?" Elsewhere Paul speaks of baptism as an experience of coming into unity through the Spirit:

> For just as the body is one and has many members, and all the members of the body, though many, are one body, so it is with Christ. For in the one Spirit we were all baptized into one body — Jews or Greeks, slaves or free —and we were all made to drink of one Spirit. (1 Cor. 12:13-14)

John Woolman used the language of baptism to refer to the experience in worship of being led into a sense of the gathered body. Here the word "baptism" implies an experience of cleansing, renewal, and a sense of immersion into the worshipping community.

> So we took the meetings in our way through Virginia, were in some degree baptized into a feeling sense of the conditions of the people. ... Through the goodness of our Heavenly Father, the well of living waters was at times opened, to our encouragement and the refreshment of the sincere-hearted. (37)

> The next day I fell in at New Garden Week Day Meeting, in which I sat with bowedness of spirit, and being baptized into a feeling of the state of some present, the Lord gave us a heart-tendering season; to his name be the praise. (149)

We visited the meetings in those parts and were measurably baptized into a feeling of the state of the Society. (108)

Such a baptism can be a painful experience because one can be led in silent worship to sense the pains of others and to bear another's burdens.

I ... was out seven days and at seven meetings, in some of which I was chiefly silent; and in others, through the baptizing power of Truth, my heart was enlarged in heavenly love and found a near fellowship with the brethren and sisters in the manifold trials attending their Christian progress through this world. (96-97)

The humility of Jesus Christ as a pattern for us to walk by was livingly opened before me, and in treating on it my heart was enlarged, and it was a baptizing time. (151)

SUFFERING

The experience of participating in the suffering of others during worship was known from the earliest days of Quakerism. Robert Barclay, for example, wrote in 1676 in his *Apology* (7:3) that the experience of the inward birth of Christ in the soul of the believer brings such a union with Christ that, using the language of 2 Peter (1:4), we become "partakers of the divine nature." Christ's obedience becomes ours, as does his righteousness, and his suffering and death. We come to have a sense of sufferings of Christ and to suffer with the Seed of Christ, the divine potential for the fullness of human life, that is suppressed in the hearts of others. We labor with the Seed of Christ for its redemption, as the apostle wrote in Colossians (1:24) that by his sufferings he filled up that which remained of the afflictions of Christ for his body, the church. Later in the *Apology* (11:7), Barclay described how in true worship a vigilant worshipper could secretly suffer, or as Friends put it, "travail" with the seed that is oppressed in another, to the edification of those present. Through our sympathetic suffering with the seed, we can serve as midwives for the birth of Christ in the heart of another. Our connection to others in the silence becomes as intimate as coaching labor.

By "dwelling deep" during worship, Friends in John Woolman's era likewise found they could come to a sense of the meeting as a whole, or to a sense of individuals in the meeting. As they came to this "feeling sense of the condition of others," they could bear the unspoken burdens of others. They could "travail" for the seed suffering in others and be like midwives in bringing this seed to birth. This silent suffering with others in worship could bring about renewal in the inward life, a renewal so powerful that they dared to call it redemptive. John Woolman put it this way:

> Christ suffered afflictions in a body of flesh received from the virgin Mary, but the afflictions of Christ are yet unfinished, for they who are baptized into Christ are baptized into his death, and as we humbly abide under the sanctifying Power, and come forth in newness of life, we feel Christ to live in us.... his spirit in the hearts of his people leads to an inward exercise for the salvation of mankind. .... Sorrow and heaviness is often experienced, & thus in some measure is filled up that which remains of the afflictions of Christ. (*479-80*)

The reason for focus here on entering into the suffering of others is to inform a later look at how this is connected with John Woolman's efforts to alleviate the suffering of those who bear the weight of oppression. Yet Quaker worship was not simply about suffering. Friends also shared their deepest joys, both in and beyond words.

MINISTRY

Discernment of the conditions of others and suffering for their spiritual benefit was the silent task of ministry. In John Woolman's words, wherever people are "true ministers of Jesus Christ it is from the operation of his spirit upon their hearts, first purifying them and thus giving them a feeling sense of the conditions of others." (31) In a similar vein he wrote, "Christ knoweth the state of the people, and in the pure feeling of the gospel ministry, their states are opened to his servants" (*314*).

For many, this corporate sense of meeting for worship has diminished in our individualistic era. But such experiences are still known. It is rather common for people who follow a contemplative practice to find themselves blessed at times with an intuitive sense of what another person might be thinking or feeling. Among earlier Friends this sense extended to the corporate life of the meeting. At other times a worshipper might sense that the community as a whole had begun to sink or center down into worship, but had not yet reached the depths that were possible. At such times Friends were known to practice what has in our day been playfully called "elevator attendant ministry." Long ago attendants in old elevators in tall buildings would call out the number of the floor as the door opened. Likewise a minister might announce that the community had begun its journey inward and downward in worship but had not yet reached the desired floor. Vocal ministry would encourage the worshippers to "dwell deep," to continue the journey toward a gathered meeting. In the 1940s Quaker writer Thomas Kelly described the gathered meeting this way.

> In the practice of group worship on the basis on silence come special times when the electric hush and solemnity and depth of power steals over the worshipers. A blanket of divine covering comes over the room, a stillness that can be felt is over all, and the worshipers are gathered into a unity and synthesis of life which is amazing indeed. A quickening Presence pervades us, breaking down some part of the special privacy and isolation of our individual lives and blending our spirits within a superindividual Life and Power. An objective, dynamic Presence enfolds us all, nourishes our souls, speaks glad, unutterable comfort within us, and quickens us in depths that had before been slumbering. The Burning Bush has been kindled in our midst, and we stand together on holy ground. (Thomas Kelly, "The Gathered Meeting," in *The Eternal Promise* (Richmond IN: Friends United Press, 1988, p. 86.)

Friends would labor in the silence to assist this experience.

Milder forms of such experience were and still are known. In Quaker meetings for worship people still often have the experience of almost rising to speak but then hearing someone else offer substantially the same message—an experience of being tuned in to the same spiritual wavelength. It is important to notice that earlier Friends did not become absorbed in such phenomena for their own sake. In their experience, the phenomena themselves were subservient to greater spiritual purposes, such as ministering to the suffering of others and assisting the community to come to a more vital spiritual life. Coming to a feeling sense of the condition of others was a divine gift, and therefore no reason to become proud. It was given to build up community and to increase love, not to make the recipient feel special and thus become diverted from the important matters in the inward life.

While we should not become distracted or preoccupied with unusual phenomena, the description of them in the writings of John Woolman and others is a useful reminder of the corporate experience of worship. This reminder can encourage us to recover that collective quality of worship, whether or not it is accompanied by intuitions of the interior states of individuals or of the collected worshippers. The gathered meeting still happens among the faithful. John Woolman enlarges this collective quality of worship to extend beyond the walls of the meetinghouse, eventually to embrace all human suffering and injustice.

Chapter 3

Scripture

The second source of John Woolman's convincement was, as he put it, "reading the Scriptures and other good books." (28) His writings are rich in biblical citations and allusions. He spoke Bible as his mother tongue, with fluency and subtlety. He found in scripture a language to describe the spiritual realities of his own experience.

THE BIBLE AS MORAL AUTHORITY

John Woolman's writings show different ways of using the Bible. Official epistles from Friends bodies are replete with biblical phrases and passages, often as supporting evidence or at least moral authority for the document's major point. (48-49, 98-101) The following is from "Yearly Meeting held at Philadelphia, for Pennsylvania and New Jersey,...1759," and regarded as the work of John Woolman.

> Our own real good and the good of our posterity in some measure depends on the part we act, and it nearly concerns us to try our foundations impartially [see Isa. 28:16, 1 Cor. 3:13, Luke

6:48]. ... We shall thus clearly see and consider that the dealings of God with mankind in a national capacity, as recorded in Holy Writ, do sufficiently evidence the truth of that saying, "It is righteousness which exalteth a nation" [Prov. 14:34]; and though he doth not at all times suddenly execute his judgments on a sinful people in this life, yet we see by many instances that where "men follow lying vanities they forsake their own mercies" [Jonah 2:8]; and as a proud, selfish spirit prevails and spreads among a people, so partial judgment [see James 2:4], oppression, discord, envy, and confusions increase, and provinces and kingdoms are made to drink the cup of adversity as a reward of their own doings [see Jer. 25:15, Rev. 16:19]. Thus the inspired prophet ... saith, "Thine own wickedness shall correct thee, and thy backslidings shall reprove thee; know, therefore, that it is an evil thing and bitter that thou hast forsaken the Lord thy God, and that my fear is not in thee, saith the Lord of Hosts [Jer 2:19]."

John Woolman also knew how to use the Bible to prove his point in disagreements, such as when in discussion of the morality of slavery.

Soon after, a Friend in company began to talk in support of the slave trade and said the Negroes were understood to be the offspring of Cain, their blackness being the mark God set upon him after he murdered Abel his brother, that it was the design of providence they should be slaves, as a condition proper to the race of so wicked a man as Cain was. Then another spake in support of what had been said. To all which I replied in substance as follows: that Noah and his family were all who survived the flood according to Scripture, and as Noah was of Seth's race, the family of Cain was wholly destroyed. One of them said that after the flood Ham went to the land of Nod and took a wife, that Nod was a land far distant, inhabited by Cain's race, and that the flood did not reach it, and as Ham was sentenced to be a servant of servants to his brethren, these two families being thus joined were undoubtedly fit only for slaves. I replied the flood was a judgment upon the world for their abominations, and it was granted that Cain's stock was the most wicked, and therefore unreasonable to suppose they were spared. As to Ham's going to the land of Nod for a wife, no time being fixed, Nod might be inhabited by some of Noah's family before Ham married a second time. Moreover, the text saith that all flesh died that moved upon the earth. I further reminded them how the prophets repeatedly declare that the son shall not suffer for the iniquity of the father, but every one be answerable for his own sins. I was troubled to perceive the darkness of their imaginations, and in some pressure of spirit said: "The love of ease and gain are the motives in general of keeping slaves, and men are wont to take hold of weak arguments to support a cause which is unreasonable," and added: "I've no interest on either side save only the interest which I desire to have in the truth, and as I believe liberty is their right and see they are not only deprived of it but treated in other respects with inhumanity in many places, I believe he who is a refuge for the oppressed [see Ps. 9:9; 103:6; 146:5-7] will in his own time plead their cause, and happy will it be for such who walk in uprightness before him." [see Ps. 84:11, Isa. 33:15] Thus our conversation ended. (63)

Note how he contrasts the "blackness" of the skin of enslaved Africans with the "darkness" of the imaginations of those who argue for slavery. Blackness of skin is no curse from God. All God's children deserve liberty. Darkness of imagination, on in other hand, is a choice to remove oneself from the light of divine guidance.

THE BIBLE AS MIRROR

Scripture was quoted, less disputatiously on the whole, in vocal ministry in meetings for worship, and on two occasions John Woolman mentions the biblical passages on which he was led to speak.

On both of these occasions, Woolman found solace in assurance of divine protection as he was preparing for his dangerous journey to the Delaware settlement of Wyalusing during a time of war. In the first he spoke on the prayer of Jesus in chapter 17 of the Gospel of John, "I pray not that thou shouldest take them out of the world, but that thou shouldest keep them from evil." (123) In the second he noted that he "was led to speak on the care and protection of the Lord over his people and to make mention of the passage where a band of Assyrians, endeavoring to take captive the prophet, were disappointed [see 2 Chronicles 32:20-23], and how the Psalmist said, 'The angel of the Lord encampeth round about them that fear him [Psalm 34:7]'" (124).

Each time John Woolman was identifying with a biblical figure, using scripture as a mirror for his own experience. Robert Barclay can offer helpful clues for understanding how Quakers read the Bible in this manner:

> God hath seen meet that herein [in the scriptures] we should, as in a looking-glass, see the conditions and experiences of the saints of old; that finding our experience answer to theirs, we might thereby be the more confirmed and comforted, and our hope of attaining the same end strengthened. (*Apology*, Proposition 3, Section 5)

To read the scriptures is to look in a mirror and find one's own inner life reflected in the lives of spiritual forebears. Reading the scriptures is an experience of growing self-knowledge. The life experiences of biblical characters are analogous to the reader's. The biblical story is recapitulated in the life of the believing reader. Each has his own exile, her own exodus. Some readers may be aware of the current renewal of *lectio divina*, or sacred reading. This is a meditative and imaginative practice of reading scripture with roots in the medieval monastic tradition. Early Friends developed their own similar approach to reading the Bible as a worshipful act.

John Woolman read the Bible in terms of his inward experiences, yet he perceived his world in profoundly biblical terms. His spiritual experiences shaped his reading of the Bible, and the Bible shaped his understanding of his experiences. He did not simply read the scriptures; he lived them. This is especially evident in his reading of the prophets.

THE JEREMIAH OF MOUNT HOLLY

Like earlier Friends, John Woolman saw himself in prophetic terms. When he searched the scriptures, he anticipated encounters with spiritual predecessors whose inward condition reflected his own. He found a particular closeness to the prophets, whose writings helped him to understand his own spiritual experience. They served as models of inward purity, which was a central concern in John Woolman's understanding of the religious life, and they called out for justice and righteousness and championed the cause of the poor and oppressed.

The biblical prophets saw themselves as maintainers of the covenant. Ancient Israel understood itself to be in a covenantal relationship with God. God would provide for the well being of the people, and they in turn would be faithful to God's will as expressed in God's instructions to Moses. These commandments shaped the relationship between Israel and God and relationships among human beings. Israelites were to be loyal to their God, which meant not serving rival deities of neighboring cultures. Ancient Israel was to build a just human society, which included honoring the rights of people outside of the centers of power and decision making. The laws of ancient Israel gave particular attention to widows and orphans, who were persons without an adult male to advocate for them in a patriarchal society, and to foreigners, who were the equivalent of what today we call immigrant laborers.

In John Woolman's day, the thought of offering sacrifices to ancient Mesopotamian deities did not entice colonial American Quakers, but he found more recent idolatries which posed a greater danger to the spiritual well-being of his contemporaries.

I believe that one Supreme Being made and supports the world, nor can I worship any other deity without being an idolater and guilty of wickedness. Many nations have believed in and worshipped a plurality of deities, but I do not believe they were therefore all wicked. Idolatry indeed is wickedness; but it is the thing, not the name, which is so. Real idolatry is to pay that adoration to a creature which is known to be due only to the true God.

He who professeth to believe in one Almighty Creator and in his son Jesus Christ, and is yet more intent on the honours, profits, and friendships of the world than he is in singleness of heart to stand faithful to the Christian religion, is in the channel of idolatry, while the Gentile who under some mistaken opinions is notwithstanding established in the true principle of virtue, and humbly adores an Almighty Power, may be of that number who fear God and work righteousness. (210)

Reflecting on the early Christians who chose martyrdom over succumbing to the command to commit idolatry, he wrote:

In the selfish spirit standeth idolatry. Did our blessed Redeemer enable his family to endure great reproaches, and suffer cruel torments even unto death, for their testimony against the idolatry of those times; and can we behold the prevalence of idolatry though under a different appearance, without being jealous over ourselves lest we unwarily join in it? (253-254)

Like the biblical prophets, John Woolman felt led to call his community back to fidelity to the demands of a covenant with God.

JOHN WOOLMAN AND JEREMIAH

John Woolman quoted many prophets, but he felt especially close to Jeremiah. Just as John Woolman bared his own inner struggles in his *Journal* more openly and more fully than most of his contemporary Quaker journalists, so Jeremiah was more self-disclosing than most other biblical prophets. Jeremiah's laments*

---

*These are found in Jeremiah 11:18-12:6; 15:10-21; 17:12-18; 18:18-23; 20:17-18.

portray the inward experience of being a prophet, and John Woolman identified keenly with Jeremiah's experience.

The similarities with Jeremiah went further. John Woolman interpreted his own historical setting as strikingly parallel to that of Jeremiah. William Penn had initiated a Holy Experiment in the Quaker colony of Pennsylvania to create a society where inhabitants could live their religion faithfully. Likewise the society of ancient Israel was a holy experiment, an effort to live out the covenant with its requirements of fidelity to God and justice among citizens. Yet in the days of John Woolman and of Jeremiah, the Holy Experiments of both William Penn's Quaker colony and the dynasty of king David, respectively, were in moral decay. Political strife and imminent foreign invasion were the order of the day. For the kingdom of Judah, the threat came from the Babylonian empire, which neither worshipped the God of Israel nor subscribed to the social justice that Israel's covenant required. For Quaker Pennsylvania, the threat was the expansion of England and France's rivalry to the American continent, and the insistence of the English crown that Pennsylvania support this war by paying war taxes and raising a militia to be ready for battle. In both Jeremiah's Judah and the Quaker colony there was a general failure of moral courage on the part of local government: Judah's King Zedekiah groveled before the Babylonian emperor Nebuchadnezzar, which inevitably meant honoring his protective deities and therefore committing idolatry. In order to raise revenues to pay the tribute demanded by the Babylonian court, Zedekiah oppressed the lower classes of his subjects. In the New World, legislative bodies in the Quaker colonies bowed to pressure to the English King George to raise taxes for war, compromising the peace testimony. In response to the threat of political collapse, both Jeremiah and John Woolman called for a return to justice and righteousness.

Questions of slavery were current in Jeremiah's time, as they were for John Woolman. Chapter 34 of the book of Jeremiah notes that Zedekiah had made an agreement with slave keepers in Jerusalem to set their Judean slaves free. The motives might have been mixed. Some may have been religious, in a genuine but belated desire to comply with the requirements of Deuteronomy 15 to set Hebrew slaves free after seven years of service. Others may have calculated that if Jerusalem were to fall under siege by the Babylonians it would be more convenient not be responsible to feed slaves, who could not work in the fields anyway during time of attack. Owners may have felt that freed persons would defend the city more vigorously than enslaved ones. For whatever motivation, they set their Judean slaves free, but only to claim them again as slaves shortly thereafter. Jeremiah proclaims divine judgment upon this reversal and re-enslavement: the God who set their ancestors free from the house of slavery in Egypt calls for their freedom. This chapter in Jeremiah must have spoken profoundly to John Woolman, the antislavery prophet of the eighteenth century.

Reading Jeremiah with John Woolman as our companion, questions arise: Is our society faithful to its commitment to justice? What are appropriate prophetic messages to our day? What forms do idolatry and slavery take in our time? Does "homeland security," for example, become an idol when it erodes the justice of civil rights?

INWARD PURIFICATION

John Woolman saw himself living in an era similar to biblical times in its unfaithfulness to God and in its sense of urgency for a message of repentance and reformation. He also identified with the prophets' experiences, internal and external.

Like the prophets, especially Jeremiah, John Woolman felt pushed into the task of calling for moral reform. Left to his own devices, he would have preferred not to put himself in situations of conflict and of confronting others. Yet he felt "under a necessity" to labor with slavekeepers, informing them of "the inconsistency of that practice with the purity of the Christian religion" (52). This purity of the Christian religion also required humility, and he looked upon his calling to defend the oppressed in ways that were uncomfortable to his own inclinations as a part of that process of purification, as it had been for the prophets:

> Through the humbling dispensation of divine providence men are sometimes fitted for divine service. The messages of the prophet Jeremiah were so disagreeable to the people and so reverse to the spirit they lived in that he became the object of their reproach and in the weakness of nature thought to desist from his prophetic office, but saith he: "His word was in my heart as a burning fire shut up in my bones, and I was weary with forebearing and could not stay" [Jer. 20:9]. I saw at this time that if I was honest to declare that which Truth opened in me, I could not please all men, and laboured to be content in the way of my duty, however disagreeable to my own inclination. (52)

Similarly, his *Journal* alludes to Jeremiah 23:29: "I was humbled before him, and at length that Word which is as a fire and hammer broke and dissolved my rebellious heart" (26).

The prophets served as models, not only of how those who are faithful to God among an unfaithful people can expect to be rejected and despised by their own community, but also as models of interior purification. They set aside their own predispositions in order to conform to the will of God. Having purified their motives, they were granted a clear understanding of God's desires for human society, namely, that people must exercise true justice and righteousness. The writings of the prophets and those of John Woolman are laden with the terms "justice" and "righteousness"—and so we see that John Woolman is also indebted to the prophets for the content of his call to reform. Yet the process of inward purification that led to insight into the nature of justice and righteousness was often a painful one.

John Woolman's experience of humiliation, of feeling disregarded because of his moral convictions and his scrupulosity, led him to look to the prophets for consolation. Jeremiah endured ridicule, imprisonment, and even threat to his life for proclaiming an unpopular message. God had made a promise to protect him and kept this promise, but often only in the nick of time. At one point some of king Zedekiah's officials had, with royal consent, thrown Jeremiah into a muddy cistern and left him there to die of hunger. A foreigner rescued him. (John Woolman would not have failed to notice that the prophet's rescuer was a black slave, an Ethiopian whose name, Ebed-melech, meant "slave of the king.") In seasons of self-doubt, John Woolman could look to these tellers of truth in costly times and find strength. He found a correspondence between their experiences and his.

FORM AND CONTENT, WORD AND ACT

The prophets offered John Woolman in form as well as content for his message. In addition to his numerous citations from the prophets, at times piled up one on another, there are times when he simply utters a prophetic oracle of his own. The language is akin to that of the prophets, but the configuration of words is his own:

> I have seen in the light of the Lord that the day is approaching when the man that is the most wise in human policies shall be the greatest fool, and the arm that is mighty to support injustice shall be broken to pieces. The enemies of righteousness shall make a terrible rattle and shall mightily torment one another. For he that is omnipotent is rising up to judgment and will plead the cause of the oppressed. (160)

There were prophets in New Testament times as well, as the apostle Paul mentioned in 1 Corinthians (12:28 and 14:1). The following quotation from John Woolman echoes prophetic language in the Epistle of James, which contrasts the friendship of God with the friendships of a human society based on injustice. Pure wisdom, which comes from God, is peaceable, gentle, and without partiality (James 3:17). God cannot, as John Woolman noted, be partial in our favor. In James, rich landowners have cheated poor laborers, and John Woolman speaks of the treatment of slaves in words echoing James 5:4, "Look: the wages of the laborers who harvested your fields, which you kept back in fraud, cry out, and their cries have reached the ears of the Lord of hosts."

> Many slaves on this continent are oppressed, and their cries have reached the ears of the Most High! Such is the purity and certainty of his judgments that he cannot be partial in our favour. In infinite love and goodness he hath opened our understandings from one time to another concerning our duty toward this people, and it is not a time for delay.
>
> Should we now be sensible of what he requires of us, and through a respect to the private interest of some persons or through a regard to some friendships which do not stand on an immutable foundation, neglect to do our duty in firmness and constancy, still waiting for some extraordinary means to bring about their deliverance, it may be that by terrible things in righteousness God may answer us in this matter. (93)

The biblical prophets did not limit their message to mere words. They performed unusual acts intended to dramatize God's message to ancient Israel and Judah. Jeremiah broke a potter's earthenware jug to illustrate the coming judgment upon unfaithful Judah (Jer. 19). He also, by divine command, buried a soiled loincloth and later dug it up, comparing its rotten state to that of Judah's moral condition (Jer. 13). To symbolize the coming servitude to the king of Babylon, Jeremiah donned a yoke on his neck and wore it in the streets of Jerusalem (Jer. 27-28). Earlier, the prophet Isaiah had dramatized the threat of the Assyrian invasion by walking the streets of Jerusalem naked (Isaiah 20).

John Woolman practiced his own prophetic acts. He wore un-dyed clothing to point out the impurity of his generation, both physical and moral, since indigo used for dyes was a product of the slave trade. Other peculiar behaviors of his included refusing to eat and drink from silver vessels, since silver was likewise a slave product. He abstained from rum and sugar because these were also the produce of slave labor. These actions were inspired by the example of prophetic symbolic behavior. John Woolman related with approval the story of a Mennonite who practiced prophetic behavior:

> At Menallen a Friend gave me some account of a religious Society amongst the Dutch, called Minonists, and amongst other things related a passage in substance as follows: One of the Minonists having acquaintance with a man of another Society at a consider-able distance, and being with his wagon on business near the house of his said acquaintance, and night coming on, he had thoughts of putting up with him; but passing by his fields and observing the distressed appearance of his slaves, he kindled a fire in the woods hard by and lay there that night. His said acquaintance heard where he lodged, and afterward meeting the Minonist told him of it, adding he should have been heartily welcome at his house, and from their acquaintance beforetime wondered at his conduct in that case.
> The Minonist replied: "Ever since I lodged by thy field I've wanted an opportunity to speak with thee. The matter was, I intended to have come to thy house for entertainment, but seeing thy slaves at their work and observing the manner of their dress, I had no liking to come to partake with thee." He then admonished him to use them with more humanity, and added: "As I lay by the fire that

night, I thought that as I was a man of substance, thou would have received me freely, but if I had been as poor as one of thy slaves, and had no power to help myself, I should have received from thy hand no kinder usage than they." (73-74)

John Woolman's unusual manners of traveling—going by foot rather than horse to meet slavekeepers and traveling to England in steerage—also are explained in part by the signs and acts of biblical prophets. Like Jeremiah and Isaiah, John Woolman intended to draw attention to the moral waywardness of his contemporaries and to call for justice and righteousness.

John Woolman's reading of the prophets helped to shape his grasp of his own leadings, his ministry, and his labors on behalf of the poor and oppressed. The prophets were a model of costly spiritual faithfulness and a source of spiritual solace as he sought to make sense of his sufferings that resulted from fidelity to his leadings. His self-understanding as an heir to the prophets was central to his identity.

Reading a passage from Jeremiah with John Woolman as our companion can open new insights. As an example, consider Jeremiah 33:14-16. These verses belong to the prophecies Jeremiah spoke after the tragic fall of Jerusalem to the invading Babylonians. Jeremiah's messages changed from warning and judgment to consolation and hope. The promise of restoration, though, did not absolve the citizens of Judah from the responsibility to maintain their covenant with God. Jeremiah 33:14-16 speaks of God's raising a righteous branch to spring up from the dynasty of David. This ruler will execute justice and righteousness. The land will live in safety, and Jerusalem will be called "God is our righteousness."

John Woolman read his own time by biblical lights. He would apply this passage to the Quaker colonies. After the wars of the 1750s peace could return to Pennsylvania, but their safety would depend on enacting justice with the native peoples of the land and justice within their borders. Wealthy landowners must stop oppressing the poor in the city, causing them to leave for the frontier and settle in lands beyond the boundaries set by treaties with the Native Americans. Like ancient Jerusalem, Philadelphia must realize that God is the source of their righteousness and their security.

John Woolman's example invites us to apply this text to our day as he would have to his. The September 11, 2001 terrorist attack on the United States was a shocking tragedy, even if it is not of the same proportions as the destruction of Jerusalem for the ancient kingdom of Judah. We need a way forward, a promise of restoration, but our safety is in direct proportion to our execution of justice and righteousness. God must supply the standard of this justice and righteousness, not an angry mob calling for revenge. John Woolman invited the wealthy in his day to compare themselves with Egypt and Pharaoh and to see the slaves in colonial America as the equivalent of the children of the Hebrews. Similarly he might invite the United States of today to compare itself not with the kingdom of Judah but instead with oppressive Babylon. In terms of size, political power, influence, and military might, the United States is closer to the Babylonian empire than to the tiny land of Judah. As the only superpower at the moment, the United States government can pursue its own policies, regardless of the advice of others. As a result, even its allies are wary. Militarily, ancient Judah could make small incursions into the territory of neighboring small kingdoms, but the Babylonian army held sway from the Persian border to the shadow of Egypt, as the United States military is currently active in Colombia, Afghanistan, and the Persian Gulf, among other places. Comparing the United States to the glorious and fiercely oppressive Babylonian empire may be an uncomfortable exercise for some, but at times prophets like Jeremiah and John Woolman deliver challenging messages.

FRIENDS AND PROPHETS

The biblical prophets were John Woolman's trusted companions in the same way that he can be a friend to a reader today. John Woolman felt known by the prophets. He found consolation in their words when his own prophetic task became burdensome. He felt challenged by them when he was tempted not to follow a divine leading. Their endurance offered him strength. He did not slavishly copy the prophets. As much as he admired Jeremiah, he did not wear a yoke in the streets of Philadelphia, or bury a loincloth, or smash pottery. Instead, Jeremiah's faithfulness to his particular leadings inspired John Woolman to be faithful to his own. This is what friends can offer one another.

One of the joys of friendship is making friends of the other friends of your friend. Reading the biblical prophets in the company of John Woolman opens a new way to understand the prophets. We can read them in his spirit. They can become our friends and can offer us comfort and challenge, just as John Woolman does. The circle of friendship widens, united by the same Spirit that offers guidance to all.

Chapter 4

Suffering and Redemption

The issue of suffering is central to all systems of religious thought. In the Hebrew Scriptures, the Book of Job stands out as an extended meditation on the meaning of suffering. In Christianity, reflection on suffering often focuses on the meaning of the cross—the sufferings of Jesus—because Christian belief holds that God through Jesus entered into human history and took on human suffering. What is more, the suffering and death of Jesus are understood and experienced to be redemptive.

John Woolman's reflections on the cross are profound because they grow out of his inward experience of participating in the sufferings of Christ. Although the historical sufferings of Jesus made redemption available for human beings, we read in the Epistle to the Colossians (1:24) that the afflictions of Christ are not yet complete. John Woolman understood this to mean that at the social level the world is profoundly unredeemed. Slavery and other forms of injustice prevail, and they cause great suffering. John Woolman felt led to enter, with the greatest respect and sympathy, into the suffering of the oppressed in order to participate in the ongoing process of redeeming the world.

Toward the end of his *Journal,* John Woolman recounts a vision experienced during a nearly fatal bout with pleurisy, a severe infection of the respiratory system. When examined in light of his other writings, this vision helps us to grasp his understanding of the redemptive work of the cross.

> In a time of sickness with the pleurisy a little upward of two years and a half ago, I was brought so near the gates of death that I forgot my name. Being then desirous to know who I was, I saw a mass of matter of a dull gloomy colour, between the south and the east, and was informed that this mass was human beings in as great misery as they could be and live, and that I was mixed in with them and henceforth might not consider myself as a distinct or separate being. In this state I remained several hours. I then heard a soft, melodious voice, more pure and harmonious than any voice I had heard with my ears before, and I believed it was the voice of an angel who spake to other angels. The words were, "John Woolman is dead." I soon remembered that I once was John Woolman, and being assured that I was alive in the body, I greatly wondered what that heavenly voice could mean. I believed beyond doubting that it was the voice of an holy angel, but as yet it was a mystery to me.

> I was then carried in spirit to the mines, where poor oppressed people were digging rich treasures for those called Christians, and heard them blaspheme the name of Christ, at which I was grieved, for his name to me was precious. Then I was informed that these heathens were told that those who oppressed them were the followers of Christ, and they said amongst themselves: "If Christ directed them to use us in this sort, then Christ is a cruel tyrant."

All this time the song of the angel remained a mystery, and in the morning my dear wife and some others coming to my bedside, I asked them if they knew who I was; and they, telling me I was John Woolman, thought I was only light-headed, for I told them not what the angel said, nor was I disposed to talk much to anyone, but was very desirous to get so deep that I might understand this mystery.

My tongue was often so dry that I could not speak till I had moved it about and gathered some moisture, and as I lay still for a time, at length I felt divine power prepare my mouth that I could speak, and then I said: "I am crucified with Christ, nevertheless I live; yet not I, but Christ that liveth in me, and the life I now live in the flesh is by faith in the Son of God, who loved me and gave himself for me" [Gal. 2:20]. Then the mystery was opened, and I perceived there was joy in heaven over a sinner who had repented and that that language *John Woolman is dead* meant no more than the death of my own will. (185-186)

For John Woolman, the meaning of the cross embraced all the figures in this vision: himself, Christian oppressors, and the oppressed who are not Christian. Applying the cross to himself, he saw it, in the language of the apostle Paul, as the death of his own will. This meant a renunciation of selfish desires that stood in opposition to pure wisdom. Applied to the Christian oppressors, the cross meant suffering with the Seed of Christ that was suppressed in slaveholders. Finally, the cross meant to enter freely into the suffering of oppressed human beings, whose cursing saddened but did not shock him because he understood why the blasphemers took Christ's name in vain. John Woolman found these three different meanings of the cross to be united in his own inner experience.

'THAT WHICH REMAINS OF THE AFFLICTIONS OF CHRIST'

Although this account of the vision is found near the end of his *Journal*, the experience occurred two years earlier. Earlier in the *Journal* he described the illness but not the vision. He wrote that he lay one night in great distress, feeling himself near the gates of death, and that he closed his eyes,

> thinking whether I might now be delivered out of the body; but in these awful moments my mind was livingly opened to behold the church, and strong engagements were begotten in me for the ever-lasting well-being of my fellow creatures. And I felt in the spring of pure love that I might remain some time longer in the body, in filling up according to my measure that which remains of the af-flictions of Christ and in labouring for the good of the church. (159-160)

The expression about the afflictions of Christ is from Colossians 1:24, the same passage Friends used to refer to expe-riences in which they came to a "feeling sense of the condition of others" during meeting for worship. This experience could in-clude suffering for the sake of others and for the Seed of Christ in them they were suppressing. In his vision, through his suffer-ing with the oppressed, John Woolman was filling up his share of that which remains of the afflictions of Christ. His suffering in the vision reflected his sufferings and labors on behalf of the oppressed. Again we see how John Woolman enlarged the concept of "a feeling sense" to embrace life beyond meeting for worship.

John Woolman believed that we can labor for the redemption of the oppressed, suffering seed—and thereby for the redemption of the oppressor. He held that the oppressor is, like the victim of oppression, also suffering, though with the important difference that the suffering is self-imposed. He expressed this in his essay "A Plea for the Poor":

> Such who are finally possessed with this selfish spirit not only afflict others but are afflicted themselves and have no real quietness in this life. (253)

To close ourselves off from God's guiding presence brings us pain. Slaveholders knew that slavery was not really justifiable morally, just as we know today that degrading the environment, for example, is inexcusable. We may try hard to rationalize such a choice: Everybody does it. It's a dog-eat-dog world. My life is complicated enough already without having to worry about one more thing. The money this brings in makes it possible for me to give my family a nice vacation. At a deeper, level, though, we are not so self-deceived. The truth gnaws at our comfort; we are not happy. When we suppress the light of God within us, we need to be redeemed from this situation.

When John Woolman traveled under the weight of religious concern to visit "such as kept slaves," these journeys had a double focus. He visited slavekeepers in order to labor with them regarding their practice of slavekeeping. His hope was both to help to bring an end to slavekeeping and to bring the captors to realize they were oppressing the Seed within themselves that was opposed to a practice so clearly contrary to truth. His intent was to assist in bringing the Inward Seed to birth in them.

John Woolman's intentions in this regard are clear from his use of the language of meeting for worship, that is, of "a feeling sense of the condition of others," to describe his visits to slavekeepers. He spoke of the need to "dwell deep [to] understand the spirits of people" while on such a journey (112).

He keenly believed that slavekeeping "deprave[s] the mind in like manner and with as great certainty as prevailing cold congeals water" and therefore can "shut up the mind against the gentle movings of uncreated purity", which bears witness against the oppressive practice of slavery. Yet there is a "witness" in others (the Seed) that one can reach. Manifesting a "spirit of true charity" is more likely to reach this witness when confronting the oppressor. John Woolman therefore wrote that Friends must "be kindly affectioned" toward slavekeeping Friends. His own descriptions of some of his visits to slavekeepers show he practiced what he preached. His *Journal* noted that "divine love and true sympathizing tenderness of heart prevailed at times in this service." When he was on another journey to visit slaveholders, we learn that "through the strength of that love which is stronger than death, tenderness of heart was felt amongst us in our visits." This is remarkable, when one considers that Woolman not only spoke to the slaveholders on a very difficult issue but also insisted frequently on paying the slaves for their services to him, as a witness against their captors to the evil of slavery (112, 237, 148, 98, 96, 102).

While traveling on foot to visit slavekeepers in Maryland, John Woolman mentioned that one of his motivations was to "set an example of lowliness before the eyes of their [the slaves'] masters." That he later states that while on this journey "the sufferings of Christ and his tasting death for every man ... was livingly revived in me" indicates he saw these labors in redemptive terms (145, 150).

PARTICIPATING IN THE SUFFERING OF THE OPPRESSED

John Woolman's inward experience of the cross included both the suffering of the oppressed Seed of Christ in slavekeepers and the suffering of the oppressed people. In his essay, "Considerations on the True Harmony of Mankind and How It Is to Be Maintained," he wrote,

> Now to those, in the present age, who truly know Christ, and feel the nature of his peaceable government opened in their understandings, how loud is that call wherewith we are called to faithfulness; that in following this pure Light of Life, we as workers together with him, may labour in that great work for which he was offered as a Sacrifice on the Cross. (*455*)

"Christ's peaceable government" is a term John Woolman used repeatedly to refer to the impetus and the goal of entering into the suffering of the oppressed (*455, 485-86*). "Christ's peaceable government" and "pure universal righteousness" were the expressions he favored to describe the social aspect of the ongoing work of redemption (*384*,157). They point to the transformation of the entire world that begins with the experience of the inward cross.

To participate in this ongoing work of the cross, one must also enter into a "feeling state of the condition" of the oppressed. The same expression John Woolman used to describe his experiences in meetings for worship is applied to his labors and afflictions on behalf of the oppressed. During his travels to slaveholders, he wrote that the "Father of mercies ... is preparing some to have a tender feeling of [the slaves'] condition," and that through the sight of oppressions witnessed in his travels, he was "brought into a feeling of the state of the sufferers" (157, 164-65). At the close of his account of a difficult and dangerous journey he made as a peace mission in a time of war to a settlement of the Delaware nation at Wyalusing, he wrote he was thankful that as a consequence of these travels he acquired "a quick and lively feeling of the afflictions of my fellow creatures whose situation in life is difficult" (137).

Later, while sailing to England, John Woolman declined to ride in the cabins and chose instead, to the dismay of many, to ride in steerage, the lower level of the ship where the sailors lodged. There he came to have a feeling sense of the condition of the suffering sailors. He wrote of God's kindness "in some degree bringing me to feel that which many thousands of my fellow creatures [the sailors] often suffer" (173). He found his heart enlarged to yearn to enter into such an understanding of all suffering people:

Desires were now renewed in me to embrace every opportunity of being inwardly acquainted with the hardships and difficulties of my fellow creatures and to labor in his love for the spreading of pure universal righteousness in the earth. (172)

John Woolman truly dissolved the walls of the Quaker meetinghouse. What he and others experienced in worship as "suffering with the suffering seed" and entering into "a feeling sense of the condition of others" he extended to life outside the meetinghouse. The intimate connection he felt to other worshippers widened to include all humankind. His inward experiences in communal worship prepared him for this, but the extensions beyond required a sensitivity, a genius, and an imagination that were uniquely his.

John Woolman's reflections on his experience of the cross reveal another motivation for some of his singular behavior, as well as for some of his travels. In addition to regarding them as prophetic signs to call the community back to faithfulness to God's desire for justice, he understood these actions as participating in the ongoing process of redemption. When he journeyed on the dusty colonial roads during the Maryland summer heat and humidity to visit slaveholders, he traveled on foot so that he "might have a more lively feeling of the condition of the oppressed slaves" (145).

To understand John Woolman's labors as efforts "to fill up that which is behind of the afflictions of Christ" is to set his famous vision into a larger, illuminating context. No longer an isolated mystical experience, it can now be recognized, for him, as the culmination and divine confirmation of his work in the ministry on behalf of the oppressed.

CLOSING REFLECTIONS

We often think of the spiritual life as essentially one of receiving. We accept the gift and open ourselves to a deeper relationship with God. Participation is different. We are not the initiators because the process is already underway; we are asked to join in a sacred unfolding. We are somehow more than recipients. Participation is itself a gift: we cannot ask for it or make it happen. Yet it cannot happen without human involvement, either. It is profoundly relational, like prayer. In fact, it is a form of deep prayer. To participate in the ongoing redemption of the world takes us to the edge of our selfhood as individual persons. The very boundaries of the self become permeable, as they can become when we have the privilege of being with someone at birth or at death. We are transported beyond the limits of our individuality to partake of something holy, something with cosmic dimensions. To bear the cross in this way is at once painful and joyful. The suffering is intense, but we do not bear it alone. We are suffered through. The power of Christ within us bears us up.

Most people do not have extraordinary visions like John Woolman's. Our own era, though, cries out for redemption at the social level. Injustice is still very much with us. John Woolman's experience invites us to see our labors for a world redeemed as a participation in the central mystery of the Christian faith, the ongoing work of the cross. John Woolman reminds us that those we identify as the oppressors also need redemption, since their lives do not show the fruits of a full conversion, which include justice. His vision invites us to act for justice out of that sacred center that we encounter in worship. Just as he beckons us to a deepening of our experience of worship, he shows us a way to be social activists whose efforts grow out of the feeling sense of the condition of others.

Chapter 5
Nurturing Empathy

John Woolman set sail for England in the spring of 1772, in what proved to be his final journey before his death in York in the autumn of that year. He spent this voyage in the part of the ship known as the steerage, the cramped quarters of the poor sailors whose life he grew to understand. His time on this ship offered him opportunity for observation and meditation. On Fifth Month 28, 1772, John Woolman wrote a rich but complex entry to his sea journal that offers readers a powerful glimpse into his inward life. This passage from his *Journal* invites us to consider how he understood spiritual transformation, to explore how he read scripture, and to reflect on the relationship between imaginative reading and imaginative ethics. For John Woolman, these three come together as "sympathy." Reading scripture under the guidance of the Spirit that gave them forth creates a sympathy, or empathy, with the biblical characters, and a sympathetic reading of scripture prepares one's heart for sympathy with others, which is the fruit of inward transformation.

Because that passage from the *Journal* is quite complex, an introduction may be helpful, including consideration of some language that may pose problems for some contemporary readers.

LANGUAGE PROBLEMS

In his vision discussed in previous chapter, John Woolman came to understand that the message of the angelic voice that proclaimed his death "meant no more than the death of my own will." (186) The expression "death of the will" is his term for a central spiritual experience, but his choice of words can seem unfortunate for some readers in our day. The expression can strike some as foreign or even frightening, perhaps with overtones of psychological unhealthiness.

This issue is important because many people have been badly bruised by life. For a long time they have wondered whether there really was a self, an integral "I" within. Perhaps a personal experience of an inward awakening to a spiritual life has given them the beginning of a sense of assurance that yes, there is a real person inside after all. Does the spiritual life order us to kill what has only recently begun to feel alive? It is important to get a better sense of how Friends of an earlier age used the word "will."

In the ideal world to which John Woolman invites readers, people should want what God wants: a peaceful and moral society, characterized by justice and equality. They should organize their lives around the experience of God's love, a love that moves us to love both God and neighbor in return. Often, however, they want something else: power, prestige, and wealth—things that they desperately hope can provide a sense of importance and permanence in the shaky existence called human life. People can choose to organize their lives around the pursuit of these goals, giving their lives a false center of gravity rather than the center that God intended in divine love.

These alternative ways of organizing human lives present a conflict. We are confronted with choice of how to orient our lives. In the language of John Woolman's day, when we want what God wants, we are conforming to God's will. When we desire what God does not, then we are exercising our own will. The problem this language presents for us is it can seem that, as human beings, we can only will what is bad. Our own will, in other words, is not a good thing. The picture of the human person that can emerge from such language can strike us as rather pessimistic. In our day we value a higher estimation of human possibilities.

But in John Woolman's day, the term "will" had, on the whole, a negative connotation. Eighteenth-century writings on education, for example, spoke of the need to break the will of a child. John Woolman did not subscribe to such ideas on education, but he did use the word "will" as his contemporaries did. We can perhaps still feel a trace of this negative estimation of the will in some uses of the word "willful" in the sense of "stubborn and unreasonable."

We might agree with John Woolman that when our desires are not centered in love of God and neighbor, we make bad decisions. When we organize our lives around fear and the construction of ultimately unreliable securities offered by power, prestige, and wealth, then we are not in conformity with God's intention for creation.

Many people of faith in our day prefer to hold on to the possibility that we can in fact desire what God desires. We want to own the choice to want what God wants. We want to define the human person in such a way that there is still an "I" who remains to make this choice. So for us, our own will is not simply the selfishness left over after we subtract what God wills. When we center our desires in divine love, we feel we are in fact affirming our truest nature. Our deepest desire, when we discern it, is what God wills.

When John Woolman speaks of the "death of the will," he does not mean murder. Spiritual growth does not imply spiritual suicide. Instead, he means a letting go of compulsive behavior that results from living our lives centered in fear rather than love. He means a release from the illusion that an incessant drive for power, prestige, and wealth affords us any final control over our destinies. For him, the death of the will is followed by resurrection into new and abundant life. This is how he understands what the apostle Paul calls dying and rising with Christ.

Just as "will" was used differently in past times, so also was the term "natural." In the New Testament, Paul contrasts the spiritually unregenerate person with the one whom the Spirit has inspired to new life. In the King James Version of the Bible, this contrast is translated as the conflict between the "natural" and the "spiritual" person. To some contemporary ears, this can sound as if people have no natural connection to the spiritual realm. John Woolman rejects such an idea and says instead that God has "placed a principle in the human mind which incites to exercise goodness toward every living creature" (25). Yet he uses

Paul's sense of "natural" to refer to the human will apart from communion with the Spirit.

For John Woolman, the way toward such communion is to set aside this natural will. The subjection of the will opens the way to freedom (or separation) from the desire for gain. This "death of one's own will" opens the way to new life, to "purity," which in turn prepares one to perceive the nature of divine righteousness and love. It is this process of transformation that is central to Woolman in this passage and that he explores in a rich, imaginative meditation on Scripture.

A TRIPLE TEXTURE

Three biblical texts provide John Woolman with the central imagery for his reflections on inward transformation. The interplay of these texts provides a complex but poetic texture.

The first is from Paul's Epistle to the Romans. In chapter 6 of that letter, Paul writes that the believer participates in the death of Christ through baptism, which crucifies the "old man" or unregenerate self. Like Christ, the believer then experiences newness of life, becoming a "servant of righteousness" (Romans 6:18).

The second focal text is from the Epistle to the Hebrews. This text sees the death of Christ as the fulfillment of what was foreshadowed in the rituals of purification in ancient Israel.

> For if the blood of bulls and of goats, and the ashes of a heifer sprinkling the unclean, sanctifies to the purifying of the flesh, how much more shall the blood of Christ, who through the eternal Spirit offered himself without spot to God, purge your conscience from dead works to serve the living God? (9:13-14)

Although John Woolman does not refer directly to Hebrews, many of the key terms in this *Journal* entry ("heifer," "purification," "figure," "reformation," and the necessity of a death) are found in the ninth chapter of the Epistle to the Hebrews. The focus of this *Journal* entry is on an inward purification, a purging of the conscience from dead works—understood by John Woolman as the unrestrained love of wealth and reputation—to serve the living God.

The final of the three focal texts is alluded to in the passage from Hebrews. It is a purification ritual from Numbers 19, in which the sacrifice and burning of a red heifer provides the ashes for what is called the "water of separation." This mixture of ashes and water purifies from sin (Numbers 19:9) and cleanses those who have become ritually impure by touching a corpse.

John Woolman interweaves these three biblical texts with others in his effort to find a way to describe what essentially lay beyond words: an encounter with the living God that results in inward death and resurrection.

THE WATER OF SEPARATION

John Woolman had been at sea for nearly a month when he wrote the entry of Fifth Month 28, 1772. His focus on the image of the water of separation may be a symbol for his own voyage, which he understood as a journey of inward purification. He explains, for example, that the leading to travel in steerage was not in his own will (163, 165). He refers to his journey as a "floating pilgrimage" that "is in some degree bringing me to feel that which many thousands of my fellow creatures often suffer" (173).

He experiences his travels on the waters of the Atlantic as yet another separation from his natural will.

In his sea journal, John Woolman has been reflecting on trade and what motivates it, on the miserable conditions of the sailors, and on the need to be "redeemed from the love of money and from that spirit in which men seek honour one of another" (173). He has been contrasting the love of God with love of gain motivated by an unrestrained "natural will." The love of God requires the renunciation of the natural will and opens the way to the "pure peaceable government of Christ" among humankind.

TEXT AND COMMENTARY

The *Journal* entry for Fifth Month 28, 1772 is quite dense. John Woolman was pushing language to its limits. The thick quilt of biblical images shows us he was reaching for all available resources to describe a spiritual experience that lay at the edges of ordinary speech. The passage begins with this central idea: When we renounce our own wills, God's wisdom puts appropriate boundaries around them. We no longer want so many things. This is an interior purification, the inward experience symbolized (prefigured, or "figured") by the ritual of the water of separation, used to cleanse someone who had touched a corpse.

> In an entire subjection of our will the Lord graciously opens a way for his people, where all their wants are bounded by his wisdom; and here we experience the substance of what Moses the prophet figured out in the water of separation as a purification from sin [Numbers 19:13, cf. Hebrews 9:9]. (175)

The red heifer that was sacrificed in the ritual prescribed in Numbers 19 brings to mind red, hairy Esau, who is remembered as a person who subordinated a Spirit-led life to his mere physical desires. This is the frame of mind that drives us toward greed. Esau sold his birthright for a paltry meal when he was hungry. He symbolizes what the apostle Paul calls the human will without the guidance of the Spirit. Elsewhere Paul calls this condition of enslavement to sin and estrangement from the Spirit "the old man." This alienated disposition leads to death, not life. But the water of separation, which symbolizes putting aside our selfish desires, is a separation from that fatal frame of mind.

> Esau is mentioned as a child red all over like a hairy garment [Genesis 25:25]. In Esau is represented the natural will [1 Corinthians 2:14] of man. In preparing the water of separation, a red heifer without blemish, on which there had been no yoke, was to be slain and her blood sprinkled by the priest seven times toward the tabernacle of the congregation. Then her skin, her flesh, and all pertaining to her was to be burnt without the camp, and of her ashes the water was prepared. Thus the crucifying of the old man [Romans 6:6] or natural will is represented, and hence comes a separation from that carnal mind which is death. [Romans 8:7] "He who toucheth the dead body of a man and purifieth not himself with the water of separation, he defileth the tabernacle of the Lord; he is unclean." Numbers 19:13 (175-176)

Greed moves us toward spiritual death, but we can be spared this death. We can be cleansed from this selfishness. John Woolman invites readers to see the reality in these biblical symbols as pointing to an inward reality that is still available. John Woolman's words invite us today to the same spiritual transformation from death to life, and he notes it may cost us the gain of our greed.

When greed motivates our pursuit of business, we are dominated by that deadly disposition, which Paul also calls "the carnal mind." In the language of the book of Numbers, we are the ones who have touched the corpse of the dead, because our selfish orientation leads toward death, away from life with God. We stand in need of the water of separation, to separate us from that selfish spirit. Yet through God's infinite love we can feel the power of Christ, as Paul puts it, to crucify us to the world. Then the love of Christ purifies us: we are cleansed in the water of separation and freed from that bondage to greed. God calls us to give up both our selfishly gained possessions and the unjust means we employed to obtain them.

> If one through the love of gain go forth into business wherein they dwell among the tombs (Isaiah, c.v.⁴) [Isaiah 65:4 via Mark 5:2], and touch the bodies of those who are dead, if these through the infinite love of God feel the power of the cross of Christ to crucify them to the world [Galatians 6:14] and therein learn humbly to follow the divine leader, here is the judgment of this world—here the prince of this world is cast out [John 12:31]. The water of separation is felt; and though we have been amongst the slain and through the desire of gain have touched the dead body of a man,

---

*John Woolman's notation "c.v." means "chapter, verse." He intended to look up this reference. In fact, the sentence conflates Isaiah 65:4 with Mark 5:2.

yet in the purifying love of Christ we are washed in the water of separation, are brought off from that business, from that gain, and from that fellowship which was not agreeable to his holy will. And I have felt a renewed confirmation in the time of this voyage that the Lord in infinite love is calling to his visited children to so give up all outward possessions and means of getting treasures that his Holy Spirit may have free course in their hearts and direct them in all their proceedings. To feel the substance pointed at in this figure, man must know death as to his own will. (176)

This "death of the will" is essential in order to see what God's nature really is. Even though we think we have understood God before, it is only when love of God and neighbor organizes our life that we can perceive the meaning of God's name as righteousness, the One who yearns for justice.

"No man can see God and live"[Exodus 35:20]. This was spoken by the Almighty to Moses the prophet and opened by our blessed Redeemer. As death comes to our own wills and a new life is formed in us, the heart is purified and prepared to understand clearly. "Blessed are the pure in heart, for they shall see God."[Matthew 5:8] In purity of heart the mind is divinely opened to behold the nature of universal righteousness, or the righteousness of the kingdom of God. "No man hath seen the Father save he that is of God; he hath seen the Father"[John 6:46].

The natural mind is active about the things of this life, and in this natural activity business is proposed and a will in us to go forward in it. And as long as this natural will remains unsubjected, so long there remains an obstruction against the clearness of divine light operating in us; but when we love God with all our heart and all our strength [Luke 10:27], then in this we love our neighbor as ourselves, and a tenderness of heart is felt toward all people, even such who as to outward circumstance may be to us as the Jews were to the Samaritans. "Who is my neighbor?" See this question answered by our Saviour [Luke 10:29-37]. In this love we can say that Jesus is the Lord [Philippians 2:11], and the reformation in our souls, manifested in a full reformation in our lives, wherein all things are new and all things are of God [2 Corinthians 5:17-18]—in this the desire of gain is subjected. And employment is honestly followed in the light of Truth, and people become diligent in business, "fervent in spirit serving the Lord" [Rom. 12:11]— here the name is opened. "This is the name by which he shall be called: the Lord our Righteousness" [Jeremiah 23:6]. (176-177)

This powerful experience of divine love brings us to commit ourselves to seeking a just human society. We root out hypocrisy from our lives, so that our actions are in harmony with our convictions. We find the strength to make necessary changes in our lives, knowing that a simple life shows our commitment to God's desire for justice and righteousness. This name of God—"righteousness"—is precious, like the ointment of the beloved in the Song of Songs. We are God's beloved, in love with the Redeemer. We know that there will be difficult changes for those of us who have accustomed ourselves to a lavish style of living that depended on injustice and oppression. We are careful not to betray the good news in such a way that anyone could misunderstand the centrality of love and righteousness in our faith.

Oh, how precious is this name! [Ecclesiastes 7:1] It is like ointment poured out [Song of Songs 1:3]. The chaste virgin [2

Corinthians 11:2] is in love with the Redeemer, and for the promoting his peaceable kingdom are content to endure hardness like good soldiers [2 Timothy 2:3], and are so separated in spirit from the desire of riches that in their employments they become extensively careful to give none offense—neither to Jews nor heathens nor the church of Christ [1 Corinthians 10:32]. (177)

In sum, when we are dominated by selfishness and greed, ultimately we are choosing death rather than life. We are estranged from God. But divine love can purify us from this polluted condition that breeds injustice. When we let go of that selfish disposition, allowing it to die, we die and rise with Christ. We then see the nature of God for the first time. God's love fills our hearts and flows from us to all people. We dedicate our lives to promoting the justice and goodness that God desires for all.

For John Woolman, divine love reorders the way we live. This wider love is prepared to take risks and to suffer. It loves the stranger—recall that this is the meaning of the New Testament word for hospitality, "philoxenia," "love of strangers"—and opens the way to a "feeling sense of their condition" in which we can imagine the life of others. This love enables us to extend the boundaries of what is called family. What Woolman here called "love" he called elsewhere "sympathy." Sympathy for others is the fruit of inward transformation, and the sympathetic reading of Scripture that he has been demonstrating in the *Journal* passage for the 28th of Fifth Month 1772 prepares the heart for this sympathy.

'A Near Sympathy'

The *Journal* entry paraphrased above offers us some important glimpses into the inward life of John Woolman. The way he used biblical materials in this passage shows us he practiced a meditative reading of the Bible. There is a powerful link between an imagination cultivated by such biblical meditation and an imagination that could radically re-envision society as more righteous and peaceable.

John Woolman's sympathetic imagination enabled him to identify with biblical events and characters, such as David (157), the prophets Isaiah (124) and Jeremiah (26), and the early Christian martyrs. His practice of reading meditatively prepared him to identify with the oppressed of his day. He used the same expression, "near sympathy," to describe his relationship with both prophets and martyrs, on the one hand, and with the victims of injustice, on the other. He was aware of the connection between a sympathetic reading of scripture and the sympathetic love for others that is the fruit of inward transformation. He speaks of "a near sympathy with the prophet" Moses (60). During his visit to the Delaware settlement at Wyalusing, he writes:

> I was led to meditate on the manifold difficulties of these Indians, ... and a near sympathy with them was raised in me; and my heart being enlarged in the love of Christ, I thought that the affectionate care of a good man for his only brother in affliction does not exceed what I then felt for that people. (134)

John Woolman, the careful editor, piled up the modifiers in that sentence. It is not simply someone's care for a family member. It is the *affectionate* care of a *good* person for one's *only* sibling in a time of *affliction*. It is, to say the least, rare for someone of European descent to express such a depth of love for the native peoples of this land in his (or, sadly, our) time.

Such sympathy was, in Woolman's understanding, originally a divine gift and a natural human inclination, yet also delicate and easily lost through inattention. The desire for riches and reputation draws us away from this sympathizing principle, but cultural conventions also play a significant role. In "Considerations on the Keeping of Negroes, Part 2," he noted that "The blacks seem far from being our kinsfolks" because of their condition as slaves. Therefore an "open friendship with a person of so vile a stock in the common esteem" would be regarded as a disgrace socially because they "have neither honours, riches, outward magnificence or power, their dress coarse and often ragged, their employ drudgery and much in the dirt, . . . so that in their present situation there is not much to engage the friendship or move the affection of selfish men." It might be like inviting the homeless into our meetinghouses and churches today. Yet, he continued, for "such who live in the spirit of true charity, to sympathize with the afflicted in the lowest stations of life is a thing familiar to them" (226). It is familiar to them because their sympathetic reading of Scripture has prepared their heart for sympathy with the oppressed.

Ultimately it is only divine love that prepares the heart for sympathy. In his essay "On the Slave Trade" he wrote, "in Divine Love, the Heart is enlarged towards Mankind universally, and prepar'd to sympathize with Strangers, though in the lowest Stations in Life" (*499*). Similarly his essay "A Plea for the Poor" states: "a person who hath never felt the weight of misapplied power comes not to this knowledge but by an inward tenderness, in which the heart is prepared to sympathy with others" (243). Yet to overcome the obstacles our culture places in the way, it is essential to use the imagination. In his antislavery essays, John Woolman encouraged his reader to "consider ourselves present as spectators" to the cruelties of slave life: our children stolen, wars in Africa promoted by the slave trade, raiding parties to carry off captives, and so on. Such acts of imagination "move us with grief. And did we attend to these scenes in Africa in like manner as if they were transacted in our presence," we would "sympathize with the Negroes in all their afflictions and miseries as we do with our children or friends" (232-233).

John Woolman prepared himself for this sort of sympathetic imagination: contrary to his own social conditioning within a racist culture, he could identify the slaves of African descent as members of his family:

> The Lord in the Riches of his Goodness, is leading some unto the Feeling of the Condition of this People, who cannot rest without labouring as their Advocates; of which in some Measure I have had Experience: for, in the Movings of his Love in my Heart, these poor Sufferers have been brought near me.

> The unoffending Aged and Infirm made to labour too hard, kept on a Diet less comfortable than their weak State required, and exposed to great Difficulties under hard-hearted Men, to whose Sufferings I have often been a Witness, and under the Heart-melting

Power of Divine Love, their Misery hath felt to me like the Misery of my Parents. (500)

He expressed the same sympathy for young slaves for whom "my Mind hath often been affected, as with the Afflictions of my Children" (*500*). Likewise he extended such loving sympathy to the oppressed sailors while on route to England: "I often feel a tenderness of heart toward these poor lads and at times look at them as though they were my children according to the flesh" (167).

John Woolman explicitly relates this sympathy to the experience of love toward all, a love which blossoms only after the experience of what he called the death of one's will. Yet we can also see how his sympathy is prepared for this by his practice of the imaginative, sympathetic reading of Scripture.

Who are today's outcasts with whom John Woolman would invite us to a near sympathy? Unemployed or imprisoned African American youth? Impoverished Afghanis and Iraqis? Persons with HIV? Undocumented immigrants who come to do work that no one else wants to do? How does our way of reading the Bible open in us a place of near sympathy for them?

Chapter 6

Engaging the World:
Practical Considerations

The works of a religious genius participate in both time and eternity. They grow out of a concrete historical setting, but they offer wisdom that transcends that particular context.

John Woolman's influence has extended beyond his life and beyond the Society of Friends. He inspired later antislavery activists, proponents of simple living and ecologically based values, advocates of war-tax resistance, and champions of social justice. The gentleness and striking degree of self-honesty and integrity in his *Journal* continue to move a multitude of readers. We find that our era faces many of the same problems. In our day, as in his, the possibility of wealth constitutes one of life's greatest temptations and spiritual dangers. Greed and xenophobia have not gone out of fashion in the wider world. Nor has racism. John Woolman's courageous imagination for a better human society and his depth of love for the socially dispossessed still inspire those who yearn for greater justice. His gifts to his readers are many-sided.

John Woolman has shown us the power of Quaker worship. He has invited us to read the scriptures anew. He has outlined an understanding of spiritual growth from the fear and mistrust of God that generates greed and oppression to the love for God and all creation that issues forth in justice and righteousness. His writings reflect on the Quaker testimonies, the ethical ideals of Friends. His writings also model how to live in such a way as to promote these ideals. His writings demonstrate practical tools for engaging the world. These practical skills are not unique to John Woolman; they are found among other Quakers and in most religious traditions. They are nonetheless an essential part of John Woolman's ministry and are helpful to those who seek to learn from him. These tools include the practice of attention to divine leadings and to our own motives, an openness to learning from those outside our immediate community, an approach to analyzing problems that is willing to see our own part in them, and engaging others so as to appeal to the pure witness of God within them.

KEEPING THE EYE SINGLE: A DISCIPLINE OF ATTENTION

The first tool is one found in all religious traditions: the discipline of attention. Even though we may truly yearn for a world redeemed from injustice, the habits of selfishness distract us and pollute our intentions. What is needed is a twofold attention, "a constant attention to divine love and wisdom," and careful observation of our own motives. Living with mindfulness of God's guiding presence and with awareness of our interior obstacles to that God-centeredness can purify the powers of perception and steady the path to righteousness.

John Woolman described how pure wisdom leads to the condition of humility, in which we accept the giftedness of life. Wisdom teaches us to trust God and to love others to the point of willingness to suffer. Pure wisdom gives us the capacity to pay attention to our motivations, so that their origin can be discerned as arising from divine love or from the selfishness that leads to oppression.

> Pure Wisdom leads People into Lowliness of Mind, in which they learn Resignation to the Divine Will, and Contentment in suffering for his Cause, when they cannot keep a clear Conscience without suffering.

> In this pure Wisdom the Mind is attentive to the Root and Original spring of Motions and Desires; and as we know "the Lord to be our Refuge," and find no Safety, but in humbly walking before him, we feel an Holy Engagement, that every Desire which leads therefrom may be brought to Judgment. While we proceed in this precious Way, and find ardent Longings for a full Deliverance from every thing which defiles, …an inward Concern is felt, that we may live under the Cross, and faithfully attend to that Holy Spirit which is sufficient to preserve out of them. (*385*)

Pure wisdom establishes the believer in love for others and incites one to work for the harmony of social justice. Wisdom's purity contrasts with the confusion of self-deception, when one is falsely persuaded that it is permissible to do what is in fact unjust. Since confusion and self-deception are is so slippery, a humble and diligent attention is needed.

> The Love of Christ, which preserves the faithful in purity of heart, puts men into a motion which works harmoniously, and in which their example yields clear and safe instruction: thus our Redeemer said, "Ye are the light of the world."

> This is the standard which God hath commanded to be lifted to the people, and the possibility of this standard being now lifted up by us, standeth in that of a lowly watchful attention to the leadings of him who is the Light of Life; and if we go from this standard, we go into a wilderness of confusion. (*472*)

Self-vigilance is especially essential for those who live in the spiritually hazardous condition of having wealth, since wealth tempts its owners to desire more wealth. During his risky journey to the Delaware settlement at Wyalusing during a time of war, John Woolman reflected on the prosperity of the English colonists and the poverty of the Native Americans forced inland from their traditional coastal lands and the oppression of the enslaved Africans in North America.

> And in this lonely journey I did this day greatly bewail the spreading of a wrong spirit, believing that the prosperous, convenient situation of the English requires a constant attention to divine love and wisdom, to guide and support us in a way answerable to the will of that good, gracious, and almighty Being who hath an equal regard to all mankind. (129)

Earlier in his *Journal* he reflected on how essential steady attention to divine guidance is, especially for the wealthy. Again, lack of attention leads to confusion. He spoke of

> an increasing care to attend to that Holy Spirit which sets right bounds to our desires and leads those who faithfully follow it to apply all the gifts of divine providence to the purposes for which they were intended. Did such who have the care of great estates attend with singleness of heart to this Heavenly Instructor, which so opens and enlarges the mind that men love their neighbours as themselves, they would have wisdom given them to manage without finding occasion ... to make it necessary for others to labour too hard. But for want of steadily regarding this principle of divine love, a selfish spirit takes place in the minds of people, which is attended with darkness and manifold confusions in the world. (55)

He called the moral confusion that results from self-deception "the secret workings of the mystery of iniquity, which under a cover of religion exalts itself against that pure spirit which leads in the way of meekness and self-denial." His *Journal* records this example, in which the practice of slavery is defended as a favor to the captive Africans.

> Another person ... mentioned the wretchedness of the Negroes occasioned by their intestine [internal] wars as an argument in favour of our fetching them away for slaves, to which I then replied: "If compassion on the Africans in regard to their domestic troubles were the real motives of our purchasing them, that spirit of tenderness being attended to would incite us to use them kindly, that as strangers brought out of affliction their lives might be happy

among us; and as they are human creatures, whose souls are as precious as ours and who may receive the same help and comfort from the Holy Scriptures as we do, we could not omit suitable endeavours to instruct them therein. But while we manifest by our conduct that our views in purchasing them are to advance ourselves, and while our buying captives taken in war animates those parties to push on that war and increase desolations amongst them, to say they live unhappy in Africa is far from being an argument in our favour." (61-62)

His desire to share the Bible with slaves is patently subversive. The reference to slaves as "strangers brought out of affliction" echoes the language of Exodus describing the enslaved Israelites. To offer the Bible to slaves was to invite them to hear a message of "help and comfort" that included the Bible's passion for justice.

Greed and oppression cloaked in the pretense of compassion are not dead and gone. Maquiladoras, factories on the Mexican-United States border, do offer higher wages to impoverished Mexicans who migrate to these border industries looking for a better economic life. Business owners are eager to point this out. Yet "if compassion...were the real motive," wouldn't they try to make it possible for their employees to have safe housing, paved roads, electricity, drinkable water, or sanitation?

John Woolman's *Journal* is open about his interior struggles to discern his motives and test his leadings. His account of the journey to Wyalusing tells of a night when the situation was increasingly dangerous and he sought guidance as to whether to continue. Once again, attention to divine leading was coupled with attention to his own possible motives.

> I had to trace back and feel over the steps I had taken from my first moving in the visit, … lest the desire of reputation as a man firmly settled to persevere through dangers, or the fear of disgrace arising on my returning without performing the visit, might have some place in me. Thus I lay full of thoughts great part of the night, … till the Lord my gracious Father, who saw the conflicts of my soul, was pleased to give quietness. Then was I again strengthened to commit my life and all things relating thereto into his heavenly hands. (130)

So he continued with his journey. At another time, he stopped a journey. He had intended to sail to Barbados, a Caribbean island with a small Quaker population and a large enslaved population. Barbados played a significant role in the slave trade.

John Woolman was packed, had left home for the port, and was ready to embark, but he was not clear as to whether he was truly divinely led to make this journey. In the end, he felt that he should not make the trip. Despite the risk of embarrassment when he returned without making the journey, he did not travel to Barbados. The *Journal* suggests that he came to see that his motives were not first of all to promote justice but instead to relieve his feelings of guilt about something he had done years before (156-158). His candid introspection revealed to him that love for others was not the primary motive. It was not a true leading. His example can inspire us as we test our leadings. Do our efforts to improve human society grow out of love or guilt?

OPENNESS TO OTHERS

Just after his description of his convincement, the passage
that states: "true religion consisted in an inward life, wherein the
heart doth love and reverence God the Creator and learn to exercise true justice and goodness," he wrote these words:

> I found no narrowness respecting sects and opinions, but believed
> that sincere and upright-hearted people in every society who truly
> loved God were accepted of him. (28)

The *Journal* later exemplifies this openness when he expressed
admiration for both Thomas à Kempis and his contemporary
John Hus. Thomas à Kempis was a loyal Roman Catholic and
was believed to be the author of *The Imitation of Christ*, a devo-
tional book highly regarded by Friends before John Woolman
and long since. John Hus was burned at the stake at the order of
Catholic Church authorities in the early fifteenth century. He
anticipated many of the teachings of early Protestant reformers,
and his martyrdom resulted from his refusal to renounce his convictions. In John Woolman's estimation, "I believe that they were
both sincere-hearted followers of Christ" (76). It was rare in the
eighteenth century for a Protestant like John Woolman to speak
so positively about a Catholic writer, but his openness to acknowledge the validity of the religious experience of others was still
wider. In his account of his sense of leading to visit the Delaware
settlement at Wyalusing, he noted:

> And in conversation with them by an interpreter, as also by obser-
> vations on their countenance and conduct, I believed that some of

them were measurably acquainted with that divine power which subjects the rough and froward will of the creature. (122-23)

The words "countenance and conduct" recall an earlier passage in the *Journal* that describes those who have been spiritually transformed.

Some glances of real beauty may be seen in their faces who dwell in true meekness. There is a harmony in the sound of that voice to which divine love gives utterance, and some appearance of right order in their temper and conduct whose passions are fully regulated. (29)

Such openness to those outside his circle was a radical break with his surrounding culture. His antislavery treatise "Considerations on Keeping Negroes (Part II)" extends this openness to persons of African descent.

There is a principle which is pure, placed in the human mind, which in different places and ages hath had different names. It is, however, pure and proceeds from God. It is deep and inward, confined to no forms of religion nor excluded from any, where the heart stands in perfect sincerity. In whomsoever this takes root and grows, of what nation soever, they become brethren in the best sense of the expression. (236)

In other words, receptiveness to this pure inward principle brings love of God and neighbor—the sum of the law and the prophets, according to Jesus (see Matt. 22:40). Convinced of this, John Woolman could write regarding the motives of his visit to the Delaware settlement:

Love was the first motion, and then a concern arose that I might feel and understand their life and the spirit they lived in, if haply I might receive some instruction from them, or they in any degree helped forward by my following the leadings of Truth amongst them. (127)

How can we come to such a place of openness? First, we see John Woolman's love for all humankind. Next, his own faith was sufficiently deep and clear that he was not threatened by the difference of others. Such openness was two-sided: he believed that an honest exchange was possible, that as a Friend he had something to offer to others. The Quaker peace testimony, which he regarded as simply the true spirit of the Christian gospel, would benefit all people. So the message of the gospel was worth sharing beyond the boundaries of cultures that identify themselves as Christian, even though many Christians did not live in accordance with "the peaceable government of Christ." Although the Light is available to all, the greed and pride that yield to war are also found in all. While he is sincerely open to non-Christians and ready to learn from them, he also knows that what he calls the peaceful government of Christ is not yet at the center of their cultures, either. To him the warring spirit was apparent in the indigenous cultures of Africa and America, as it was in his own. So-called Christians who kept slaves, stole land from and cheated Native Americans, or oppressed the poor were not yet redeemed from greed and pride. They did not yet know that universal love toward all. They did not yet know "salvation in [Christ's] name." In John Woolman's experience, the essence of the Christian message of salvation was a changed heart. Those who have experienced this redemption are eager to share it, as John Woolman sought to share it among his fellow Quakers and other Christians. He was a missionary to those whose Christian conversion was incomplete, whose redemption was unfinished. Instead of oppressing others, stirring up the warring spirit within us all, and provoking them to war and violence, believers ought to offer them the merciful spirit of peace that lay at the heart of the gospel. To do this with integrity requires first of all a major transformation within those who profess to be Christian. It requires the experience of inward death and resurrection described in Chapter 5.

DEALING WITH CONFLICTS

As we have seen, John Woolman was frequently led to take the unpopular side in a controversial issue. He gave literally decades of his life to the cause of ending slavery, particularly slaveholding by his fellow Quakers. He labored to bring yearly meetings to clearness on the evils of slavery and to minute that clearness, when it finally came. When the English and French extended their rivalries to the North American continent during the Seven Years War, he opposed the payment of war taxes, a minority view among Friends at that time. So, John Woolman often went about his ministry anticipating conflict. His advice on dealing with disagreement continues to be as timely as it was in his day. Here are some of his principles.

1.   Do not pretend the conflict is not there.

It does no good to avoid conflict, papering over it as if it were not there. This is dishonest and ultimately destructive of friendship, of trust, and of community. When in conflict, both parties need first to acknowledge it and then work to resolve it.

> To see the failings of our friends and think hard of them, without opening that which we ought to open, and still carry the face of friendship—this tends to undermine the foundation of true unity. (112)

Often it is hard to acknowledge the conflict because we disagree sharply about things that, in the larger scheme, seem so trivial. We tend to fight about the color of the new carpet in the worship room or what message we should put on the answering machine. A member of my meeting put it this way: "We squabble about little things. While that's annoying, it is also reassuring because it shows that we agree about the important things." Yet we can also be deeply divided over major issues, such as how to respond collectively to a member's inappropriate behavior. In many meetings and churches there are deep theological differences, but we are afraid to confront this reality. The example of John Woolman can give us courage to face our differences.

2. Value real community.

Like his contemporaries, John Woolman placed a great value on community. The community was where the leadings of the Holy Spirit were discerned and where gifts in ministry were recognized and publicly acknowledged. True ministry arises from the center but happens only in community: one's ministry begins in one's own community and from there travels out, with the blessing of the home community. Even when John Woolman had to wait for most of the rest of Quakerism to catch up with him on many controversial issues, he continued to believe that the gathered body open to divine guidance was the place where wisdom becomes incarnate. He cared enough for his own community to seek patiently to teach it. He was not the sort of purist who chose schism and separatism as the solution to a community that does not always live up to its ideals. The individualism of our era has made it even more difficult to value community. Each meeting and church has its stories of struggle to tell.

3. Keep your eye single to righteousness, not self-image or self-righteousness.

Purity was a focal concern for John Woolman, but it was not a purity that worried most of all about keeping his own hands clean. He readily admitted his part in the injustices of the world, but this did not lead him to a paralyzing guilt. It led him instead to focus on those injustices and how to play a role in bringing about their transformation. The great thing about this focus is that it freed him from self-righteousness—an enormous temptation for the morally sensitive. Just as a misplaced concern for appearances can tempt us to ignore conflict, so likewise an overgrown concern for our individual appearance as a good person can pose a significant obstacle to resolving differences.

4. Move beyond merely blaming others.

Because we are all so connected, and because we all fall short of our ideals, it is unwise and untrue simply to blame others as wrong. Often we are a piece of the problem. When Native Ameri-

cans on the western frontier of Pennsylvania sided with the French
and began to attack English settlements in the war of the mid-
1750s, city dwellers were quick to blame western settlers. Some
of them had laid claim to lands not included in treaties, and some
had cheated Native American fur traders and sold them rum to
great harm. John Woolman described this wicked practice viv-
idly.

> I perceived that many white people do often sell rum to the Indi-
> ans, which I believe is a great evil. First, they being thereby de-
> prived of the use of their reason and their spirits violently agitated,
> quarrels often arise which ends in mischief, and the bitterness and
> resentments occasioned hereby are frequently of long continuance.
> Again, their skins and furs, gotten through much fatigue and hard
> travels in hunting, with which they intended to buy clothing, these
> when they begin to be intoxicated they often sell at a low rate for
> more rum; and afterward when they suffer for want of the neces-
> saries of life, [they] are angry with those who for the sake of gain
> took the advantage of their weakness. Of this their chiefs have
> often complained at their treaties with the English. (125)

John Woolman does not deny these evils but also pointed
out that urban landowners were not so innocent themselves.

> Where cunning people pass counterfeits and impose that on oth-
> ers which is only good for nothing, it is considered as a wicked-
> ness, but to sell that to people which we know does them harm and
> which often works their ruin, for the sake of gain, manifests a hard-
> ened and corrupt heart and is an evil which demands the care of all
> true lovers of virtue to suppress. And while my mind this evening

was thus employed, I also remembered that the people on the frontier, among whom this evil is too common, are often poor people, who venture to the outside of a colony that they may live more independent of such who are wealthy, who often set high rents on their land, being renewedly confirmed in a belief that if all our inhabitants lived according to sound wisdom, labouring to promote universal love and righteousness, and ceased from every inordinate desire after wealth and from all customs which are tinctured with luxury, the way would be easy for our inhabitants, though much more numerous than at present, to live comfortably on honest employments, without having that temptation they are often under of being drawn into schemes to make settlements on lands which have not been purchased of the Indians, or of applying to that wicked practice of selling rum to them. (125-126)

He was not satisfied to analyze this injustice as only the problem of someone else who was conveniently out of sight. He was not afraid to see himself included in his analysis of social problems. In the midst of a reflection on the need for the wealthy to live "in that humility and plainness which belongs to a Christian life, …thus lead the way to a right use of things" so that justice might prevail for the poor, he did not absent himself from the picture. He acknowledged that he had in his own way contributed to the problem by his own desires that required immoderate labor.

And as I have thus considered these things, a query at times hath arisen: Do I in all my proceedings keep to that use of things which is agreeable to universal righteousness? And then there hath some degree of sadness at times come over me, for that I accustomed myself to some things which occasioned more labour than I believed divine wisdom intends for us.

In order to work, this principle of moving beyond blaming others requires the previous principle of focusing on doing the good thing rather than on looking good. We can become frozen in feelings of guilt if we acknowledge our role in the evil in the world and still fret about our self-image. John Woolman would agree with Martin Luther's great insight that we contribute to the sinful condition of the world and yet God is ready to accept us. When we open ourselves to this acceptance, we feel free from the need to impress anyone anymore. We do not need to impress God because we have accepted the fact that God has accepted us. We no longer need to impress ourselves or others because we realize we were trying to substitute that for the acceptance from God. This is tremendously liberating. It gave John Woolman courage to wear undyed clothing or ride in steerage. It can give us strength to follow the leadings we receive from God.

Elsewhere he noted that these "imaginary wants," which exceed the bounds of pure wisdom and which he confessed to having, lead eventually to war itself. The passage begins by contrasting human greed with the habits of creatures regarded as less intelligent than human beings but which nonetheless do not desire more than they need:

Hath he who gave me a being attended with many wants unknown to brute creatures given me a capacity superior to theirs? — and shown me that a moderate application to business is proper to my present condition, and that this, attended with his blessing may supply all outward wants while they remain within the bounds he hath fixed, and no imaginary wants proceeding from an evil spirit have any place in me? Attend then—O my soul!—to this pure wisdom, as thy sure conductor through the manifold dangers in this world.

His queries continue, describing the progression from vanity to greed to oppression, and finally to war.

Does pride lead to vanity? Does vanity form imaginary wants? Do these wants prompt men to exert their power in requiring that of others which themselves would rather be excused from, was the same required of them?

Do those proceedings beget hard thoughts? Does hard thoughts when ripe become malice? Does malice when ripe become revengeful, and in the end inflict terrible pains on their fellow creatures and spread desolations in the world?

Yet this progression can be stopped—and he admonishes himself to remembrance of the divine source of peace and that following Christ means living simply, which opens the way to peace and shuns greed and oppression.

Does mankind walking in uprightness delight in each other's happiness? And do these creatures, capable of this attainment, by giving way to an evil spirit employ their wit and strength to afflict and destroy one another? Remember then—O my soul!—the quietude of those in whom Christ governs, and in all thy proceedings feel after it. ...Remember, O my soul, that the Prince of Peace is thy Lord, that he communicates his unmixed wisdom to his family, that they, living in perfect simplicity, may give no just cause of offense to any creature, but may walk as he walked. (142-143)

John Woolman's astute analysis of the inward progression from greed to anger to vainglory is reminiscent of the acute observations of ancient Christian monastic literature. Writers from the fourth and fifth centuries such as Evagrius Ponticus and John Cassian were similarly discerning in their observations of the state of the soul and the influence of greed, anger, pride, and other inward motions. Where John Woolman differs is in his movement beyond the individual person to the effects on wider human society. Again we see the integrity of the inward and outward life.

5.   Strive to reach the pure witness in others.

Within the human heart there is found what Friends called "the pure witness." Of divine origin, it testifies to the truth of what lies before it. When the pure witness within us is reached, we are open to spiritual growth, ready to receive what to us is new truth. In the language of John Woolman, our hearts are enlarged in love and our minds are purified to understand the true nature of righteousness (176-177). The Spirit of God can lead us into truth and into unity when we are truly open. We can become bearers of that truth for one another, but this is a delicate task. If we feel led to be such bearers, particularly on controversial matters where there is not unity as to the nature of what is just or right, then we must speak in a way that invites genuine listening.

Feeling ... a renewed concern that the pure Principle of Light and Life, and the righteous fruits thereof, may spread and prevail amongst mankind, there is an engagement in my heart to labour with my brethren in religious profession, that ... [we] may so walk that our conduct may reach the pure witness in the hearts of such who are not in profession with us. (475-76)

Genuine humility and charity must characterize the labors of those seeking to convince others of the need for social change to bring about justice. John Woolman was not the only Friend in his day opposed to slavery. He knew of others whose harangues against Quaker slaveholders had little effect in changing them. The eccentric if committed abolitionist Benjamin Lay was eventually disowned for his outrageous behavior to dramatize the evils of slavery. Once, during yearly meeting sessions, Benjamin Lay stood up and denounced slavekeepers.* The cruelty of their slaveholding, he said, was as immoral as thrusting a sword through the slave's hearts. He removed his plain Quaker greatcoat, revealing a military uniform. He unsheathed a sword and thrust it though a hollowed out book, in which he had hidden a bladder of scarlet berry juice. The "blood" splattered on those nearby. He had a flair for the dramatic.

Despite Benjamin Lay's passionate devotion to ending the evils of slavery, others felt that his motives were mixed. He seemed to enjoy shocking others for the effect itself. He liked drawing

---

*Robert Vaux, *Memoirs of the Lives of Benjamin Lay and Ralph Sandiford; Two of the Earliest Public Advocates for the Emancipation of the Enslaved Africans*, (Philadelphia: Solomon W. Conrad, 1815), pp. 25-27.

attention to himself. Rather than attract others to the good that they might do, his actions simply labeled others as evil. His actions shocked others but failed to inspire them to change. John Woolman may have hinted at this kind of motivation when he wrote:

> If such who were at times under sufferings on account of some scruples of conscience kept low and humble and in their conduct manifested a spirit of true charity, it would be more likely to reach the witness in others, and be of more service in the church, than if their sufferings were attended with a contrary spirit and conduct. (98)

That spirit that reaches the pure witness in others is a spirit of peace:

> O how precious is the Spirit of peace! How desirable that state in which people feel their hearts humbly resigned to the Lord, and live under a labour of mind to do his will on Earth as it is done in heaven. Where ... true love so seasons their proceedings, that the pure witness is reached in such who are well acquainted with them. (401)

Like Benjamin Lay, some people today are so zealous to be at the cutting edge of any issue that they seem unconcerned as to who it is that gets cut off along the way. Zeal is not known for its patience, resulting in unkind grumblings and accusations of stalling and maneuvering against sincere people engaged in an honest searching of their souls. Whatever one's inclination on a controversial issue, it is painful to watch see others unvalued as they are still struggling to find their way. This kind of zeal fails to cherish community.

In the experience of John Woolman, righteousness and love are inseparable. Justice and righteousness are what love of God and neighbor look like. They are the shape that love takes when it is lived out. When we allow ourselves to be touched by the Spirit of God, "a tenderness of heart is felt toward all people, even such who as to outward circumstances may be to us as the Jews were to the Samaritans" (177). When our concern for justice and righteousness are firmly grounded in universal love, we can stay centered in that love when controversy arises. A measure of the universality of John Woolman's love is that he was able to love those whom it is often hardest to love: members of his own community with whom he strongly disagreed.

THE POWER OF EXAMPLE

Words are powerful means in the effort to persuade others to change, but example is even mightier. For John Woolman, an example was not simply an illustration, nor was it merely a tactic used to convince others in an argument. Example had a spiritual power of its own to influence the hearts and minds of others, in ways that they might not even consciously recognize at first.

An analogy for John Woolman's understanding of example might be the doctrine in the eastern Orthodox Christian churches regarding icons. An icon is an image of Christ or the saints for veneration. In traditional eastern Orthodox teaching, the icon participates in the spiritual reality that it is seeking to portray.

The spiritual realm stands behind the icon, ready to invite the viewer into that reality through the material substance of the icon. The icon appeals to the physical sense of vision, but Orthodox theology teaches that there are also spiritual senses, aroused through appeal to the physical senses. An Orthodox monk once playfully told me, "Icons are postcards from heaven: 'Wish you were here!'" An icon has the power to summon the viewer into spiritual transformation. Although Quakers have abstained from sacred art, John Woolman believed that virtuous people share in a similar power. Their virtue participates in the goodness of God, and their example has the capacity to invite those who see their example to spiritual transformation. Through them God is reaching out to others, and the witness of God in the hearts of those who see them confirms that such virtue contains truth.

John Woolman's understanding of the spiritual power of example is akin to his understanding of the power of imagination to transform, both in reading Scripture and attending to its images and in imaginatively entering the suffering of the oppressed. Perhaps here is where Quakers, while formally non-liturgical, manifest the same spiritual impulse that finds expression in liturgy in other Christian bodies. The language of partaking of divine life is common to all these religious experiences.

> Where people are sincerely devoted to follow Christ and dwell under the influence of his Holy Spirit, their stability and firmness through a divine blessing is at times like dew on the tender plants round about them, and the weightiness of their spirits secretly works on the minds of others. (68)

Many of us have met people like this. They have a spiritual presence about them that gently invites us to be better people. Their centeredness in divine power exerts an influence on us in ways that we may not even be aware of at the time. Such a person for me was Barbara Reynolds. Her unshakeable faith, her spirit of hospitality, and her commitment to a world without war gently drew me into the Quaker fold. Barbara went to Japan on behalf of the United States government after the atomic bombings to research the effects of the bombings on Japanese society. Her experiences there convinced her to devote her life to preventing another atomic tragedy. I met her many years later, when she was nearing retirement age and I was a college student. I would join her and others for meeting for worship at her house on the edge of campus on weekday mornings before rushing off to German class. The memory of her still blesses me, nearly thirty years later. I invite you to remember someone who has touched your life with grace.

Negative examples also hold power, so John Woolman repeatedly warned of this danger. Evils such as slavery can clothe themselves as socially acceptable and thereby work great harm. Like violence in the media or pornography in our day, the effects, he realized, were often unconscious yet real and demonstrable. He meant to counter the effects of negative examples with the power of good example in his own life, and here we may find yet another motivation of his striking prophetic behavior.

John Woolman's travels to slavekeepers show his efforts to reach the pure witness in the slaveholder by the power of example. We might imagine the scene and its effect on the slaveholder. First the slaveholder, as a proper host, welcomes John Woolman and offers to send one of his "servants" to care for John Woolman's horse. His guest explains that he has traveled to Maryland from New Jersey on foot—because if he were a slave he would not have a horse. Taken aback but still the polite host, the slaveholder then offers his guest some refreshments. After all, he has been on his feet a long time. John Woolman quietly tells him that his conscience cannot allow him to use his host's silver because silver was mined by slaves. So the host finds substitute drinking vessels, and then asks John Woolman if he takes sugar in his tea. His gentle guest declines—sugar is a product of slave labor. Opening formalities concluded, the conversation begins in earnest. John Woolman tells of his leading to travel in the gospel ministry, to visit "such as kept slaves" to persuade them of the evils of slavery. He wants the slavekeeper to understand that slavery is not only bad for the oppressed slaves but is dangerous to the spiritual well being of the slaveholder and his family. John Woolman's concern embraces oppressor as well as oppressed. Finally, the difficult conversation over, John Woolman takes his leave, but first he leaves money to pay the slaves for their labor! Throughout this exchange, his humility and charity have shone forth. These have not hindered the power of his message. On the contrary, they have enhanced it. By his example he has tried to reach the pure witness in others.

THE EXAMPLE OF CHRIST

The best example of humility and charity is Jesus himself, who, Christians believe, partook fully of the divine life. This life showed forth to others in his earthly ministry, appealing to the pure witness in them. Although he was the eternal Word through whom all things came into being, the one who was "the Son of Him who is greater than earthly princes . . . became a companion to poor, sincere-hearted men" rather than seek out the company of the powerful. When on trial and facing the sentence of death,

> though he signified to Peter that he had access to power Sufficient to overthrow all their outward forces; yet retaining a resignation to Suffer for the Sins of mankind, he exerted not that power, but permitted them to go on in their malicious designs, and pronounce him to be worthy of death, even him who was perfect in goodness. (*448*)

This profound humility, as Woolman points out, extended to the act of forgiveness at the moment of greatest suffering:

> It was for our sakes that "he was put to grief; he was wounded for our transgressions; he was bruised for our iniquities" [Isaiah 53:5] and under the weight of them manifesting the deepest compassion for the instruments of his misery, laboured as their Advocate, and in the deeps of affliction, with an unconquerable patience, cried out, "Father, forgive them, they know not what they do." [Luke 23:34] (*448*)

Because scripture has issued forth from the inspiration of the Holy Spirit, when someone reads scripture under the divine guidance, the "pure witness" of the Spirit within her or him convinces the reader that it is true.* Further, the power of the example of Christ's humility moves the reader to imitate Christ's ideal of a plain and simple life that is not dependent on the oppression of others to provide luxuries.

His essay "On the Example of Christ" is John Woolman's extended meditation on the apostle Paul's description of the self-humbling of Christ in Philippians 2, which Paul prefaces with the admonition, "Let this mind be in you which was also in Christ Jesus." Looking to the humility of Christ as the example, Woolman writes:

> Now this mind being in us, which was in Christ Jesus, it removes from our hearts the desire of Superiority, worldly honours or greatness. A deep attention is felt to the Divine Counsellor, and an ardent engagement to promote, as far as we may be enabled, the happiness of mankind universally. (*448-49*)

He notes that those who have in them the mind of Christ "feel a tenderness of heart towards those of low degree." They seek to lead others out of the entangling customs of the world regarding the pursuit of wealth and reputation. They look "into

---

*John Woolman read this in the *Apology* of Robert Barclay, who in turn got it from his reading of John Calvin. See Barclay's *Apology* 3:1, where he quotes John Calvin's *Institutes* 1:7.

the wants of the poor," and "hold forth such a perfect example of humility, that the pure witness may be reached in man's minds, and the way opened for a harmonious walking together." This is in part what is implied in being a co-worker with Christ in the ongoing labor of redemption. It is also a succinct description of John Woolman's understanding of his own labors in the ministry.

> Now to those, in the present age, who truly know Christ, and feel the nature of his peaceable government opened in their understandings, how loud is that call wherewith we are called to faithfulness; that in following this pure Light of Life, *"we as workers together with him,"* may labour in that great work for which he was offered as a Sacrifice on the Cross, and that his peaceable doctrines may shine through us in their real harmony, at a time when the Name of Christianity is become hateful to many of the heathen. (*454*)

Christ's peaceable doctrines must shine through the lives of those whose hearts have truly been changed, and so John Woolman travels to Wyalusing during the dangerous conditions of war in order to cherish the spirit of love and peace among the Delaware people, travels on foot to visit slavekeepers in order "to set an example" of this meekness before their eyes (145), and sails to England in steerage to dramatize how the greed of ship owners brings oppression to sailors.

"On the Example of Christ" concludes with the hope that the example of Christ will continue in his disciples, reaching the pure witness in others.

the believers of Christ may so abide in the pure inward feeling of his spirit, that the wisdom from above may shine forth in their living, as a light by which others may be instrumentally helped on their way, in the true harmonious walking. (*449*)

John Woolman's concept of example sheds light on his purposes in writing his *Journal* and essays. His intent was to serve as an example, to appeal to the pure witness in his readers, and to invite them into the inward transformation that he experienced. By the spiritual power of imagination, John Woolman's readers are summoned to participate in the ongoing work that was his life.

Closing Thoughts

To Take Heed
to Our Own Spirits

J ohn Woolman's writings are always in season. Yet now is an especially important time to listen to John Woolman. His writings give us one of the best models, after Jesus, for how we find hope in the present chaos and find ways to act to improve our world. These times call for change at a deep place within ourselves. John Woolman shows us the courage to accept change within, and we see the blessed results in his life.

It is my hope that these essays have encouraged you to begin a friendship with John Woolman, one that will grow and develop. A friendship with him can change your life, if you are open to grace. Reading John Woolman as a friend, we can admire his deep dedication to justice. His decades-long work to end slavery can inspire us to stay with the causes to which we are led. His perseverance can strengthen our resolve. We can take encouragement from his frank self-revelations. Despite his admirable ideals, he was not perfect, as he repeatedly confessed in his writings. His candor can give us hope because we also profess high ideals in spite of our imperfections. John Woolman does not give us the excuse to set him on a pedestal as a life to which we can never hope to attain. He shows us his human-ness in all its dimensions, and these very shortcomings give the rest of us hope.

John Woolman offers himself to us as a companion when we read the Bible. Reading the Bible as he did, we can see it as the language of the inward landscape. We can open ourselves to the depths of personal transformation, knowing that the shape of our ministry will be different because our strengths and limitations are different from his, and our times are different. John Woolman would not want us to copy him with unthinking admiration. Reflecting on his concern to refuse to pay war taxes, he noted that was not a leading of earlier Friends, but it was a legitimate concern for his historical context. He wrote that "It equally concerns [people] in every age take heed to their own spirits" (84). Truth continues to unfold. As one generation is faithful to the light given it, the way opens "for sincere hearted people to proceed further afterward." He saw "a gradual progress from age to age" (147). His era could not be concerned, for example, with HIV; ours must be.

We can be grateful for his enduring insights into how to work with others to achieve positive change. At the same time, since honest friends acknowledge their differences, we might agree to disagree with him on some issues, such as the understanding of the relationship between human will and God's will, or on how to work most effectively for change in our complex, global economy. Or singing in a choir.

We can thank our friend for the invitation to revitalize our worship. We can emulate his integrity of the inward and outward life. We can read John Woolman's writings again and again, to revisit a dear friend and to deepen a precious relationship.

Group Discussion Guide
Introduction

This is a discussion guide for Chapters 1-6 of *A Near Sympathy*. Each of the six sessions begins with a gathering thought, which could be read by the group leader at the beginning of each session or as a shared ministry by a different member of the group at each session. Allow a few minutes of quiet gathering/worship after the reading.

The questions that follow the gathering thought are intended as triggers for your discussion. It is not necessary to discuss every question. You may find one question that draws deep response or interest and decide to spend the entire session on it. And, participants may raise other issues from the chapter for discussion.

You will notice that one question for each chapter is starred. We suggest participants spend time during the week before the discussion thinking about this question in particular, noting at least their initial responses.

Chapter One

GATHERING THOUGHT:

> "Where the heart was set on greatness, success in business did not satisfy the craving, but that in common with an increase of wealth the desire of wealth increased." (35)

Where are you on the contemplative-activist continuum? How do you feel about those who are elsewhere?

Have you had a turning point experience in your religious life? How would you describe true religion?

What is love like for you? Have you experienced the different kinds of love that John Woolman describes?

What are your feelings about work? Do you work too much?

*Most of us want things that we do not really need? Can you identify any in your life? What might it look like to embrace a simpler life?

What role might the imagination play as a spiritual discipline in your life?

Chapter Two

GATHERING THOUGHT:

"The outward modes of worship are various, but wherever [people] are true ministers of Jesus Christ it is from the operation of his spirit upon their hearts, first purifying them and thus giving them a feeling sense of the condition of others." (31)

What is worship like for you? Can you describe some experiences that have had a special meaning for you?

*In what ways has worship helped you to experience a sense of connection to others? Does John Woolman open any new possibilities for you?

What might it be like to "dwell deep" in worship?

Reflect on these words from the apostle Paul: "For in the one Spirit we were all baptized into one body — Jews or Greeks, slaves or free — and we were all made to drink of one Spirit." (1 Corinthians 12:13) What meaning do they have for you?

Chapter Three

Gathering Thought:

> "The messages of the prophet Jeremiah were so disagreeable to the people and so reverse to the spirit they lived in that he became the object of their reproach and in the weakness of nature thought to desist from his prophetic office, but saith he: "His word was in my heart as a burning fire shut up in my bones, and I was weary with forebearing and could not stay." [Jer. 20:9] I saw at this time that if I was honest to declare that which Truth opened in me, I could not please all men, and laboured to be content in the way of my duty, however disagreeable to my own inclination." (52)

Can you read the Bible as though it were a mirror? What have been your experiences of exodus? To what have you been in bondage but are now set free by God?

How do you feel as you read the biblical prophets? Are you in some way called to live a prophetic life?

Are there biblical characters with whom you feel a closeness, as John Woolman felt with the prophet Jeremiah?

*Choose a passage from scripture and imagine reading it in the company of John Woolman. What new insights do you find?

Chapter Four

GATHERING THOUGHT:

"The Lord in the Riches of his Goodness, is leading some unto the Feeling of the Condition of this People, who cannot rest without labouring as their Advocates; of which in some Measure I have had Experience: for, in the Movings of his Love in my Heart, these poor Sufferers have been brought near me." (500)

What might it mean for you to fill up according to your measure that which remains of the afflictions of Christ?

Have you ever felt a sense of the sufferings of the oppressed? What was that like?

Spend a few moments in reflection on these words from the apostle Paul: "I am crucified with Christ, nevertheless I live; yet not I, but Christ that liveth in me, and the life I now live in the flesh is by faith in the Son of God, who loved me and gave himself for me." (Galatians 2:20) What might this passage mean for you?

*Think of social injustice that troubles you. What would it be like to try to relate to the oppressors as John Woolman did with the slavekeepers?

Chapter Five

GATHERING THOUGHT:

> "I was led to meditate on the manifold difficulties of these Indians, ... and a near sympathy with them was raised in me; and my heart being enlarged in the love of Christ, I thought that the affectionate care of a good man for his only brother in affliction does not exceed what I then felt for that people." (134)

Would you agree with John Woolman regarding the need to be "redeemed from the love of money and from that spirit in which men seek honour one of another?" What in our culture poses an obstacle to that redemption? How would you describe the way forward beyond those obstacles?

In this chapter, John Woolman is striving to describe a fundamental spiritual transformation. What for you is interior transformation? How would you describe the process that brings people to love for all?

What might it be like to try to read the biblical passages that John Woolman draws on in this chapter as he read them? Are there other passages that for you offer deep resources for describing the movement from fear and greed to love?

*Have you had any experiences of what John Woolman calls "near sympathy?" How would you describe them?

Chapter Six

GATHERING THOUGHT:

"Where people are sincerely devoted to follow Christ and dwell under the influence of his Holy Spirit, their stability and firmness through a divine blessing is at times like dew on the tender plants round about them, and the weightiness of their spirits secretly works on the minds of others." (68)

How do you exercise the discipline of attention? Are there spiritual practices that you find especially helpful? How do you seek to discern the truth when you are confused?

Describe some experiences when you have been open to people outside your particular circle or tradition.

Can you tell of some experiences when you faced a conflict even though you may have been strongly tempted to avoid confrontation?

Share some stories of times you have tried to reach the pure witness in others. Do you have any success stories?

*As you finish reading this book, what conversations would you like to have with John Woolman?